AGNES:
HOW MY SPIRIT SURVIVED

AGNES: HOW MY SPIRIT SURVIVED

by AGNES SASSOON

LAWRENCE COHEN LTD.

First published 1983 by
Lawrence Cohen Ltd. 297 Hale Lane,
Edgware, Middlesex.

ISBN 0 9508834 0 9
and ISBN 0 9508834 1 7 (Cased Edition)

Printed by De Mandus Print Limited,
Barnet, Herts.

Contents

Foreword

The horrors of war are, alas, always with us, either as a shattering personal experience or hanging over us like a dark threatening cloud. Why then add to the miseries of the human lot by recalling the horrors of nearly forty years ago?

Agnes Sassoon, a victim of the Belsen atrocities, approaches the subject from a new angle: how the human spirit is able to withstand 'man's inhumanity to man' and still remain human. The controversial TV film 'Holocaust', she says, showed us as soulless and mindless bodies. The victims were portrayed as shells with no feelings. Agnes wrote this book to give humanity back to the people who 'walked like shells'.

I was with the British Second Army and served with a Brigade whose forward troops entered Belsen camp in April 1945, when the terrible conditions first came to light. Agnes was in that camp. After hospital treatment she was transferred to Hanover where she stayed for a few months of rehabilitation with a group of other inmates of the camp. I got to know her well after hostilities ceased because, along with several other Officers of my Regiment, we arranged gramophone recitals, theatre visits, dances, swims — anything which would help the process of healing and readjustment to normal life again.

The conditions in Belsen were so appalling and almost unbelievable that it was decided there and then to record them for all time. This documentary evidence, supported by gruesome photographs, was printed in Germany, and I have one of the original copies. The atrocities are now part of man's awful history. What is not so well known is the unquenchable human spirit which the Nazis tried to crush, but failed. Agnes Sassoon exemplifies this unquenchable spirit.

Geoffrey Lesson, M.B.E.
(Formerly Captain, Royal Artillery)

Editor's Note

A chance telephone call brought me into contact with Agnes Sassoon when she rang the newspaper for which I worked, to invite the writer of "The Women's Page" (me) to a buffet lunch and fashion show to be held at her home. I helped serve the lunch and immediately struck up a rapport with Agnes. A few weeks later she invited me again to lunch saying she wanted my opinion on something. Intrigued, I accepted, and while Agnes bustled about the house, I started reading a bunch of typed papers which she had casually asked me to look over. I suddenly lost my appetite. I was reading about a child who was thrown onto a pile of dead bodies, presumed dead, a victim of the insane Nazi "Final Solution". But no — this couldn't be Agnes! This mercurial woman whose zest for life made you want to gasp for breath, this couldn't be the same person whose skeletal body I was now reading about! Of course — it was. Did I perhaps know of anyone who might be interested in helping to correct the manuscript for her, in a style which could be identified with that of a young girl experiencing the horrors of Nazism, yet without losing the emotions and feelings of a human being who had not lost hope or vision? I was hooked! My decision to help (after Agnes had approved my style) was the first step in a series of events which were to change *MY* life.

It was not an easy task as Agnes and I worked together on the original manuscript trying to ensure that her story written in her mother tongues translated faithfully into English but finally the job was done and as so often happens in life the reward was unexpected and greater than ever imagined. Agnes and her husband brought me to Israel for a holiday, then twelve months later, at a time when I was emotionally distraught and in need of a change of scenery, I returned to Israel and fell in love — on two counts. I fell in love with Israel, and met a man who was to give me back my love of life. (My marriage had ended some two years previously, and the devastation I had experienced almost cost me my life). Agnes was "chapter one" in what I call "My second life".

Agnes, a remarkable child with the will to survive, became a remarkable woman. This is her story......

Sylvia Hebden.

Introduction

So many books have been written, both fact and fiction, about the atrocities committed by the Nazis during the last war that many people may wonder why I decided to have this book published. Why now so many years after the war ended?

Initially my writing began when I was actually in the concentration camps, but it was writing with a difference. It was virtually impossible to obtain or keep anything from the vigil of the German soldiers. The odd scraps of paper and bits of pencil I occasionally found were soon discovered and taken from me, followed by the reprimand and flogging which had become part of my life. So I had to improvise my writing materials, and thus my brain became my pencil, and my memory became the paper on which I wrote. Or, to update it slightly, my brain dictated to my memory incidents and happenings to be recorded like words on a tape which could be played back time and again as required. The need for this "writing of the mind" arose from the unnatural environment in which I found myself. When work or the pace of life becomes too much in normal circumstances people can relax, take a break, go on holiday or simply read a book; anything to take their minds off present problems. For us in the concentration camps there was no respite from the horror of our surroundings, no refuge or retreat to which we could withdraw. We had no privacy, no possessions and no peace from the constant roll-calls, searchings and beatings. The only way I could "switch off" from all that was happening around me was by engrossing myself in the task of writing. So, I dictated to my memory. Years later, when I went to Israel, those memories helped me to earn a living, for I began writing of my experiences for newspapers and magazines. But why this book?

Some time ago, a programme was shown on television which created a mild stir. It was called "Holocaust". As a result two things were impressed on my mind. One was the apparent ignorance of today's youth about the events of four decades ago and two, the reactions of my own two sons, then aged sixteen and twenty. Pictures were shown of camp inmates looking like walking skeletons, of bodies piled one on top of the other awaiting the ovens, of pits and trenches filled with the skeletal corpses. After watching scenes like this my own sons voiced their disbelief. "Mummy, we can't believe that you lived like that or looked like that. If it were so, you wouldn't be alive today".

So, 35 years after I was freed from this living hell, I decided to tell my story. I want people to know that we were not mindless bodies. We may have looked like corpses, but we still had emotions with which to feel and brains with which to reason. If we closed our minds, it was to try to make our suffering less. Of what use was it remembering the past with its comforts and happiness, its food and affluence, when we were dying of hunger, disease and torture? Some people have a greater tolerance of suffering than others, a greater willpower and determination to survive. One third of the Jewish population was wiped out — over six million victims. In total, Hitler slaughtered an estimated thirteen million men, women and children in his bid to create a "racially pure" Germany. This is the story of one who survived.

I dedicate this book to my own two sons, and to the sons and daughters of the world, that they may read and believe that it DID happen, that they may learn from what happened, and that they may determine that it will never happen again.

I would like to acknowledge the encouragement and assistance given me in researching the historical background to the early chapters by the late Dr.L.Veress, the former Hungarian diplomat, broadcaster and historian. He helped me to fulfil my dream and I will always revere his memory.

Agnes Sassoon

CHAPTER 1

I Meet Hitler

I was about five and a half years old, the daughter of a Jewish school teacher, living with my parents in Bratislava when Munich sounded the death knell for Czechoslovakia. I was attending German kindergarten to learn the language, for at that time it was customary for middle class families to have their children learn several European languages even at Nursery School. One day, in the late Autumn of 1938, we were told at school to prepare ourselves for the arrival of a very important person. He was to visit us the following day, and we were all instructed to wear German national costume in which to greet him. It was to be a special day for everyone. It certainly seemed special to me, for although my German classmates had ethnic dress as a matter of course, I did not. I gave my mother quite a time, insisting that she make me the required blouse, apron and dirndle skirt, otherwise I would not be allowed to attend the important gathering and meet the special celebrity. Adolph Hitler had just annexed Petrlźalka (Grünau), a Danube bridgehead facing Bratislava, and had come to visit his new conquest. It was there that we crossed the bridge and assembled to greet him on this very special day. He drove by slowly, followed by his retinue, standing in his car with arm raised in salute. He stopped before the youngest children, stooped over his car, and with the help of his companion officers lifted up a child who was standing in the crowd holding a bunch of flowers. He raised the child above the car, kissed him and set him down again. Had I been closer to the car that child could just as easily have been me. He then addressed the school dignitaries: "Are there any

Jewish children left? They must all be removed at once". I heard the words, but at the time did not grasp their significance. So it was, from Hitler's own mouth, that I received my marching orders. The very next day I was removed from the German school and transferred to a Jewish one — but not for long. My parents were soon obliged to leave Slovakia and sought safety in Budapest. The first stage of our life in Hungary lasted from 1939 until March 1944.

In Budapest we lived under sufferance. In order to survive my father had to sell his valuables. He still had his diplomas and was able to obtain part-time employment teaching maths and physics. At first we had a passable life as my father's position carried with it a certain amount of respect, but later he was dismissed because of his religious affiliations. Through influential friends he obtained a post at the Research Institute which delved into people's backgrounds and origins to prove whether or not they were Hungarian-born Jews. These researches could save lives by delaying the deportations, depending on what information was discovered and passed on. The job itself paid little, but for my father the rewards were great. He could help save innocent lives. From other odd jobs which he undertook my father eked out a living for me, my older brother and my mother. He became involved with the underground movement, helping to save the lives of Jew and Gentile alike by falsifying documents and information at the research centre. It was a difficult time for my parents but they did what they could to keep my brother and me cheerful and away from trouble. During the school holidays they would send us to stay with our grandmother who had a vineyard in one of the border villages where conditions were easier. There we would help tread the grapes for winemaking and we became friendly with the village peasants. Even the local police were more liberal in their attitudes, so life was pleasant for us during those visits. We always ate better when we stayed with our grandmother and she would give us food to take to our parents for the return home. I remember those holidays as being happy times. Later, the Jews of that village were herded into ghettos, where they lived miserably until their departure for the camps. After our last holiday there I never again saw my grandmother or aunts and uncles from that village.

I attended a Jewish school during that uneasy period of our lives, which ended so dramatically in March 1944 when Hitler marched into Hungary. Then the persecution of the Jews began with a vengeance.

We were obliged to move into a "yellow star" house set aside for Jews. We were made to wear yellow stars to distinguish us, making us easily-spotted prey for the Arrow Cross (Fascist) hunters. We were subjected to limitless restrictions and constant humiliation, and could be stopped and searched at any time in any place. Adolf Eichmann himself, one of the arch organisers of the holocaust, came to supervise the deportations of the Jews from the provinces; we in Budapest had a stay of execution. My father risked his life by forging and obtaining "safe conduct" Aryan documents and French diplomatic protection in "safe houses" for Jews in hiding. He never wore the yellow star himself. We lived in constant fear, the children quickly learning not to scream out or cry when the soldiers approached. Like frightened mice we would scurry to our parents, afraid to speak or move.

Admiral Horthy, the Regent of Hungary, tried to make peace on October 15th, 1944, but was removed from office by the Germans and replaced by the Arrow Cross regime which took command of Budapest. Then began the third, most terrible phase of my life. The hitherto protected Budapest Jews were herded into ghettos and the deportations to the German death camps commenced. The Arrow Cross soldiers killed Jews in the streets and hung them for all to see, in their homes, on the roadways; men, women, children, babies. A public proclamation was issued that the life of a Jew was without value. Cold calculated murders were committed daily and no-one could or would stop them. The jackboot had arrived and life in Budapest would never again be safe for a Jew. Food was already rationed and in short supply, but more so for the Jews. Some shopkeepers refused to serve Jews even when they were entitled to rations.

Our "yellow star" home consisted of two rooms and a kitchen. We had no bathroom and the toilet was outside. Basic items like sugar and eggs which we had considered necessities became luxuries which were not afforded to Jews. My father continued to help smuggle people to safety and our home was a constant refuge for the fugitives. I remember it as a terrifying time; never knowing when our home might be searched, despite all the precautions we took to conceal our flow of "visitors". Even a trip to the outside toilet was a security risk! Every day was filled with tension and uncertainty. I knew that we lived in constant danger, but I never really understood why. Was it wicked to be a Jew? Why did people avoid us and call us names? Why did my friends no longer want to play with me, and why did we have to speak in whispers? Then, my childish innocence could not understand; today, despite my experiences, such behaviour is still beyond comprehension.

My brother, three years my senior, was sent away to live with a "safe" family. False Aryan papers had been obtained and the family was well paid for their trouble. Twenty four hours later my brother was back with us much to the distress of my mother and father. He could not stand the fighting and foul language which passed between the grown-ups and their children. He begged my father to put him to work, anything rather than return to that dreadful house. So, my father went to see his friend at the French Embassy, a Mr. Henri Ader, a man he knew to be sympathetic to the cause and probably, like my father, a member of the underground movement. He advised that my brother be sent to Moszar Street 3, where Zionist and Gentile groups arranged safe hiding for people on the run. My brother was sent to join a fairly large group of fugitives, but they were betrayed, and marched at gunpoint to the banks of the River Danube. There, along with the rest of the prisoners, he was shot dead, and his body pushed into the watery depths of a mass grave. At about the same time, unaware of the murder of my brother, I was being herded along with others to begin my tortuous journey which would eventually lead me to Dachau. A cruel twist of fate allowed my father to save the lives of so many but denied him the ability to save his own family.

CHAPTER 2

The Death March

Just how fortunate it was that there was no need for my mother to see me to and from school became apparent that dread day in November. The "permitted" school at the local synagogue was attended by all those Jewish pupils who had been refused entry at their normal schools by the Nazis. If my mother had made an exception on just that one day, she may not have survived long enough to help me tell this story.

Until the "putsch" of October 1944 it was still safe — even for a girl with a Yellow Star — to walk to and from school alone, though only of course at the permitted times. After that date we became fair game for the Arrow Cross headhunters or the SS so we had to be prepared for the worst at all times. With the onset of those chilly wet November days, my mother sent me to school dressed in several layers of warm clothing, well protected against the harsh elements of the Hungarian winter. I wore strong sensible shoes too, strong enough to withstand the many miles of walking which I would have to endure, though as yet I had no inkling of my fate.

We came out of school between one and two o'clock in the afternoon. School finished early in those days because of the air-raids and the curfew, and we all streamed out anxious to heed our parents' pleas to arrive home as quickly as possible.

As soon as I reached the front exit I had one of those dreadful sinking feelings which one cannot always explain, and saw across the road a number of trucks and the green-shirted Arrow Cross squadmen waiting in the street, guns at the ready. To overwhelm a group of defenceless children the Fascists had not only surrounded the buildings with their own troops but had also despatched a large number of German SS soldiers to supervise the operation. I had seen this all too familiar sight before and instinct told me to escape, but there was no way out. Everyone who crossed their path was seized — parents anxiously waiting to escort their children home, even a middle-aged woman who was wearing a Yellow Star and just happened to be passing. After they had rounded up those children outside, the Arrow Cross hooligans burst into the school, smashed all the equipment and dragged out at gunpoint those terrified children who had run back inside to hide.

At eleven years of age, I must have been one of the youngest pupils. The sufferance that had been extended to our little school had abruptly come to an end.

We were all herded into the waiting trucks. I found myself next to the woman who had unfortunately crossed the square at the wrong time. She must have taken a liking to me as she smiled at me gently as if in sympathy for what lay ahead. Seeing me hesitate over which of the trucks to enter — orders were for the children to travel together — she took charge of me and guided me to the truck carrying the adults. She told me that her name was Aranka, and she advised me to stay with the grown-ups and say that I was four years older than my real age, should I be asked. Obviously she had no illusions about the fate of children being deported to the camps: an eleven year old would be sent straight to the gas chambers for extermination; a fourteen or fifteen year old would be kept alive to be used as slave labour. My childish instinct told me to listen to Aranka, and I stayed as close to her as I was able. She was a blonde, somewhat buxom woman, perfectly groomed and obviously quite wealthy. I noticed her elegant finger nails, well manicured and varnished bright red, and her beautiful face. A woman of intelligence, she appeared to be acting as mother to me, something I was to be grateful for both then and in years to come. She undoubtedly saved my life with her advice about my age.

The Arrow Cross men threatened us to keep us all quiet, but we were so conditioned that it did not take much for us to remain silent lest we endanger the lives of others. When she could, Aranka tried to reassure me by saying that they would be taking us to some pleasant place where I would eventually meet up with my parents. She was trying to make the ordeal easier for me, but I just knew that this was not the truth. Instead, we were first driven to some horrible brickyard on the outskirts of Budapest. Some of us were left in the open under the wintry November sky which was gradually growing darker. There were just a few makeshift tents for shelter. I was hungry, cold and dazed, but I dared not complain. I just stayed as close to Aranka as possible, determined not to be separated from her. We were kept there for what seemed to be days as others joined us, until we were numbered in thousands. Somehow, I became separated from the others I knew, but I remained all the time with Aranka who continued to keep a motherly watch over me. I was a tiny figure lost in a crowd of desperate people torn from their loved ones. What was to be our fate? Most able-bodied Jews had already been rounded up for "forced labour" or had had the foresight to go into hiding before they were hounded by the Nazis. So when the Germans called for fifty thousands Jews to work on the construction of a line of fortifications or in labour camps in Germany, the Arrow Cross obliged by seizing women and children from the streets or from their homes. Thus I became a member of the labour force for Hitler's Reich at the tender age of eleven.

Once again we were herded into the trucks, this time

to be taken to a sports ground in Budapest, the main deportation centre to the camps in Germany. More days passed by, days which we spent in the open, without any kind of shelter or sanitation, and at the mercy of the freezing winter weather. Sometimes we were served a thin, watery soup, but as I had no dish, I had to miss out even on this doubtful form of nourishment. I had not yet learned the art of survival, so it had not occurred to me to find some form of container to use as a soup bowl. About four days later Aranka and I were ordered to join a column setting out on a long march. There was no indication of where we were going to or of how long the journey would take. We were made to walk on roads, tracks or footpaths, across the cold wet Hungarian countryside. We were driven along by blows and curses from the Arrow Cross guards who seemed to take delight in kicking or beating those who faltered and could not keep pace with the rest of the contingent. Many fell by the wayside, from weakness and exhaustion, and were usually shot in full view of everyone else. At night we stopped at farms or sports grounds where we rested and slept; sometimes in the open, sometimes, if we were lucky, in barns or hastily erected shelters. For food we were given the inevitable watery soup and a piece of bread, the latter always hard and, more often than not, mouldy.

One scene from that terrible trek remains firmly and indelibly fixed in my mind. We were passing through a town when we came across some form of procession. Men were carrying a Roman Catholic hierarch dressed in full ecclesiastic garb, with great pomp and ceremony. As the holy marchers passed us, they paused, while their revered charge gave us his blessing. I heard his words spoken in the name of God, but heard no words of protest in the name of humanity. Someone whispered that this was Cardinal Mindszenty, but I was too young to know and the name held no meaning for me. I knew only that he was someone of importance by the crown and red and gold robes which adorned him. His holy blessing gave us little comfort. It felt more like the blessing given a condemned man awaiting death at the gallows.

We were compelled to continue our weary shuffle. I was stopped by what appeared to be a kind elderly guard who whispered this advice to me. "Escape little girl. I won't look, I shall turn my back. Try to get lost". Perhaps he really meant it and had suddenly felt a prick of conscience for a little child, knowing what fate lay ahead, but some instinct told me that his advice was not sound. After all, I did not know where I was. Where would I go and how would I get back to Budapest? In any case after days of marching on meagre rations I was in no fit state to be wandering around the countryside taking chances. Besides, I wanted to be with Aranka, for I felt a certain security as long as I remained close to her. Our march progressed at a pace towards the Austrian border. By rail or road this would have been a distance of about 115 miles, but it seemed that with all the detours the journey was twice the distance. We were cold, hungry, exhausted and weakened by the time we — the survivors that is — arrived at the Austrian frontier. Many who had not kept pace with us had been shot or beaten up and left for dead. A few had slipped away unseen by the guards. Maybe they survived. More likely they were recaptured and shot. By this time Aranka, so smartly dressed at the beginning of our journey, looked dishevelled, neglected and sick. I tried in my childish way, to give her some of the comfort she had given me, and I put my arms around her, as I had done on happier occasions with my dear mother. I noticed that through her beautifully groomed blonde hair, the white was showing, and her nails, so elegantly polished before, were chipped and broken. Her face seemed to crumble in despair, and she suddenly looked very old.

Thousands of other victims from Hungary and other parts of Hitler's empire were gathering at the frontier. They had preceded us, and as they stood there awaiting their next move, they stared at us with dead expressionless eyes. Eventually we were all moved onto railway shuntings where we again waited, no-one knew why or for how long. Later we were moved and driven into railway wagons — the sort that usually transport animals — which were part of a long train. Some of the wagons were open-topped, some closed. The Germans had purloined whatever was available and crammed us in about seventy to a car. Conditions were indescribable — today there would be an outcry if animals were transported in such a fashion.

Somehow, during this confused period of shunting and waiting, I became separated from Aranka. I looked desperately at the faces of my companions, needing the security of that one person in whom I could trust. Though I searched time and again during the ensuing days and weeks I did not find her. I shall never know whather Aranka died then or survived to tell her own story.

The journey was interminably long — longer than my estimated time of the march. I am sure that it took us not only across Austria, but also across a sizeable part of Germany. From listening to the grown-ups I began to think that perhaps even our guards did not know the destination at which they would at last be able to dump us. How we survived the train journey I shall never know for the Allies were constantly bombing the railway. Later I was to wonder whether or not they knew that these trainloads were carrying thousands of unwitting victims to the concentration camps.

I was so conditioned to the swaying of the train and of people collapsing around me that I jumped with surprise one wintry morning on hearing the sound of much shouting whistling and clanging. Our train had halted on the track in sinister desolate country covered with a veil of snow.

"Raus, raus" barked the guards, and we climbed down from the wagons, fearful of what lay ahead. Some were so weak and ill they could hardly muster the energy to move, but they were helped down by the guards who gave them a swift kick and a blow on the head. More guards were waiting for us with dogs and we were driven through a gate which bore the inscription "Arbeit macht frei" — "Work achieves freedom". We had arrived at the gates of Hell — the concentration camp at Dachau. Along the tracks I saw corpse-like bodies shovelling away the snow. With outstretched hands they begged us for our bread ration which we had received at the border. Having made the gruesome journey before us they knew that we would have bread, a treasure more precious than gold to a starving man. In my innocence, believing that I would soon be given proper food, I gave my portion to a man close by before passing through the gates of my new home.

CHAPTER 3

Alex Petrushka

After the arduous ugly and degrading journey from the Austrian frontier, I was devoid of feeling. I had spoken hardly at all during the journey, I had just been waiting for it to end, hoping for better conditions when and wherever we arrived. The section of Dachau where I was dumped was called "Landsberg 11" as I remember it. Not that the name mattered or that I could have cared much at the time, as I was in a state of complete exhaustion. I was reduced to skin and bones after the wanderings of the past weeks. However, resembling a skeleton actually worked to my advantage; there was no way of telling how old I was. Without documents or identification papers to give me away, it was possible for me to follow Aranka's advice and add a few years to my age. Under normal circumstances at eleven years of age I might have been very much a child, but since the age of six, when I had become aware of the meaning of fear, I had grown wiser and older than my years. Now, I felt more like an old woman than a girl on the threshold of her teenage years.

We were herded to a block where new arrivals were supposedly "deloused", given a shower, had their hair shorn and were then compelled to change into prison garb. All clothing had to be removed. I took off my sturdy shoes, my warm overcoat, woollen dress and underwear in which my mother had sent me to school some weeks before. They were now worse for wear and scruffy but still better than the clothes in which I had seen the inmates dressed.

In the "changing room" I first set eyes on Alex. He too was an inmate. It was impossible to tell his age because of his emaciated condition. He must have been much older than I, but I could see that he was still quite young. His skin was like alabaster and his face shone with some translucent whiteness. A pair of very dark sad eyes was the dominant feature of his face, and on his head he wore a warm woolly cap pulled well down over his ears. He was tall, and like everyone else there, skeleton-thin. His ragged coat bore his number both back and front. I was not permitted to stand and gaze at Alex for we were pushed into the "delousing room". Here I was overcome by a fit of hysterical crying which soon spread to the other women inmates. It was uncontrollable, a blockful of women all crying and sobbing. The SS guards rushed in wielding their rubber trucheons and bludgeoned us into silence. I thought that I would surely not survive their terrible blows as they beat me about my head and shoulders.

I saw that Alex was looking at me with profound compassion, and I could see tears in his big dark eyes. I felt that he was concerned for me and I realised that his feelings were not yet completely destroyed. At first sight he had seemed devoid of emotion, but something had touched him now, and I recognised the flicker of warmth which passed across his face. I felt an instinctive "togetherness" and knew that I should stay close to him for safety and protection. His years of experience in the camp at the mercy of the Nazis had taught him what could happen to inmates who disobeyed orders or had hysterical outbursts likely to influence or disturb the rest of the prisoners. It seemed to me that his eyes were trying to tell me not to cry — for my own safety.

Alex's job was to distribute clothes and footwear to the new arrivals. He did so mechanically and dispassionately, without saying a word, conditioned to the task he had performed so many times before, year after year. To me he gave a thin cotton smock which was split at the back. It was so worn that normally it would have been used only as a rag for cleaning. For footwear I was given two totally unmatching evening shoes. One was high heeled, the other flat, and they were of different sizes. Of course, neither of them fitted as they were intended for adults and my own feet were indeed very tiny. I was expected to walk the snow-covered barrack yard and work in these shoes. Altogether, I must have looked unspeakably grotesque. I was utterly miserable. Where were my parents? Aranka had kept me quiet by saying that they would be waiting at the end of my journey. What was I doing here in a dreaded camp with people I did not know, all much older than me? My one grain of comfort was that Alex managed to speak to me a little while later — at much risk to himself. The sorrow I thought I had seen on his face earlier when he spotted me had been real. I had reminded him of himself, of the day when he had arrived at Dachau — a child like me. Alex told me he had been in the camp since he was ten years old. In fact, he was one of the first inmates of Dachau concentration camp. Dachau had been established as early as 1933 and the camp had mushroomed to accommodate the vast numbers of people who were to pass through its portals. The world had refused to believe that any nation could contemplate anything so inhuman as the concentration camps, and the reports filtering from Germany at that time had gone completely unheeded by many of the leading statesmen and governments. Alex must have spent nearly eleven years in that camp and was about twenty-one when we first met. I learnt of his life and circumstances which had brought him to Dachau in the precious stolen minutes we used to share whenever we could meet. Each meeting was dangerous for us both, but the strength of our attachment outweighed the danger involved. Instinct told me to have full confidence in Alex and I told him my real age. We formed a deep mental attachment which helped make our wretched existence just a little more bearable. Our meetings were brief and dangerous — a few minutes snatched when no-one was looking. We had to be extremely cautious, for if we had been discovered we would probably have been shot on sight or at least severely beaten. Somehow, Alex managed to manoeuvre these few moments together and they gave me hope for the future.

Alex's surname was Petrushka and during our times together he told me what had happened to him and his parents. His father had been a first class musician of Polish origin who had lived most of his life in Germany. A Jew himself, he had met and fallen in love with a non-Jewish German girl. After Hitler's rise to power she had been confronted by the authorities and given a choice; either she must immediately divorce her husband or else face the consequences of having married into that despised people. Theirs was a true love match and she refused to leave her husband. She had spoken up bravely — too bravely, in fact, for the liking of the SS. They dragged her from her home and shot her in front of her then ten-year old son, Alex. Alex and his father were seized and sent to Dachau, the first camp to be established. As the Reich expanded and the concentration camps multiplied, they were separated and his father was later despatched to Auschwitz where he most probably was added to the evergrowing list of Nazi victims. Ten years in the hands of the Nazis was quite a record, and Alex had survived merely by the tolerance of a succession of SS officers. During this time, his status could only be described as that of a pet monkey. It was a situation which he hated but one nonetheless to which he owed his life.

Having been raised in Germany and being half German, Alex spoke high German like a native. He had inherited his father's musical talents and played the violin well. In Dachau the German officers made him play whilst they guzzled their food and swilled down their beer and spirits. They affected an air of culture and sensitivity when listening to him play, and seemed to be deeply moved by his renditions of certain pieces by Brahms and Mozart. As reward they would throw him scraps of food from their plates as one would do to a pet dog. During the day he was kept busy in the store room giving away the clothes of dead inmates to new arrivals. Like the rest of the prisoners Alex was not spared the blows and kicks of the guards. However, he had an existence. The guards had their entertainment and may even have felt sorry for him in their fashion.

Undoubtedly I owed my own survival to having stated my age as fourteen. I spoke German fluently and I was capable of working. Sometimes I worked in the kitchens for the SS guards. Even though we were driven like slaves and everything was scrutinised for the least little mistake, it was warm there and preferable to working outside in the cold. Mostly it was due to Alex that I was able to work inside. At the end of each day the men and women would be separated and herded off to a sleeping block where a regulation number of inmates would huddle together on one continuous wooden bunk. Any form of comfort was out of the question, even for our rest periods, and the bunks were hard, overcrowded and uncomfortable. Sleep came about through sheer physical and mental exhaustion, and most people were too ill to care about the hardness of their beds.

During this time it was Alex who kept my spirit and soul alive. I owed my will to live to the moral aid and comfort which he gave to me at every opportunity during our brief meetings. In the absence of some sublime word I can only say that our affection grew to a youthful, pure but naive love. During our brief periods together, we talked and made plans for the future. He taught me the art of survival and how to steal food when the opportunity arose. He told me never to be greedy and take too much, for that would endanger my life. I must not take a whole potato — just a little of the skin. A tiny piece could be hidden under a belt or a waistband without detection. A crumb of bread was better than nothing at all and would not be found if I was searched. However tiny the scrap I could steal it would help me survive just a little bit longer. I took note of all he told me, respecting his knowledge and experience and grateful for his friendship. We talked about what would happen to us after the war and I told him that he would come to live with me and my parents for I firmly believed that they would still be alive, yet equally certain that Alex's father would have perished by now. Because I did not know of physical love, apart from my parents' and relatives' embraces, I regarded him as one would a brother. He would be my new brother and my parents would look after him too; this I believed with all my heart.

The one personal possession that Alex had succeeded in keeping was a gold medallion which his mother had given him as a gift. This, his most treasured possession he handed to me. What deep feeling I experienced I cannot put into words. I was overwhelmed that he had chosen to give me his last material contact with his past. Miraculously, I too succeeded in keeping it, hiding it sometimes under my tongue, sometimes on other parts of my person. Much later, on a train on my way back from Germany to Prague, it was taken from me. Most of the travellers on the train were soldiers, and many other passengers, like myself, had their possessions taken from them. I lost more than a medallion that day.

I began to look upon my life in the camp as a daily fight to survive. Each day I awoke was a miracle renewed. Malnutrition, lack of hygiene and inhuman living conditions were taking their toll and were decimating the ranks of the inmates. I saw before me so much suffering and sorrow, so many old people dying of starvation or freezing to death through exposure and maltreatment. I was taken ill with typhoid fever but somehow struggled on. Anyone who was likely to spread the epidemic was thrown into the dreaded black van and transported to the gas chambers or directly to the ovens, thus reducing our numbers in yet another way. Under the circumstances Alex made superhuman efforts to preserve my life. He smuggled his own weekly ration — always in short supply — into the block where I was lying in a delirious state. Somehow, none of the inmates noticed my condition, perhaps because everyone else was in a similar state, and most people were indifferent to the needs of others anyway. Even the camp superintendents failed to notice that I was sick, and they could have at any time condemned me to death. Alex pressed his own meagre rations on me, supplemented by the scraps thrown to him by the Germans as he played for them whilst they ate. At first, I refused to accept his food, perhaps because at the time I thought his chances of survival were greater than mine. He pleaded and pleaded "Take it, you must if you have any thoughts for me. I have nobody in the world left but you". I did not know how, but he even managed to steal some milk for me — I had forgotten the taste and it was like having the sweetest, most precious nectar.

One night he slipped into the block with another life-saving crust of bread. In whispers we spoke of the future and about all the happy things we would do and share together. He told me he had heard one of the SS guards saying that the future was not too hopeful for Hitler and the forces of the Third Reich, and that the war would soon draw to a close. "If only" he said, "we can survive another few weeks. That's all it needs Agnes. We may yet see freedom again and of course we must stay together, always''. I trusted and believed in his words and again we started to make plans. We each hoped for the other, and our words comforted us in that bleak prison. Much as I wanted him to stay with me, I urged Alex to leave. The risk he took in visiting me was a constant worry. It needed only a word from one of the inmates, perhaps hoping for a reward of extra food, and Alex would be in mortal danger. Others in my block were well aware of his gifts, of his love and caring for me, and human nature being what it is, jealousies were aroused. He had already stayed with me longer than usual and it was now dead of night. The only sounds were the moans of the inmates and the thud of the guard's footsteps. Alex slipped out of the window. As practiced as he was, he was unable on that night to evade the beam of searchlight from one of the watchtowers. The beam alighted on the window — and on Alex. I held my breath, frozen in terrified anticipation of what might happen. Alex jumped quickly out of the window but he had been spotted. A machine gun rattled and I saw Alex fall. Without even considering what would happen to me I rushed out and took his warm hand in mine; perhaps he was still alive. Sobbing, I searched for a spark of life from my Alex not noticing the SS guards who ran towards us. The blows from their truncheons rained on me but I felt no physical pain whatsoever. I was quite oblivious to their savage kicks and beatings as I clung to Alex and cradled his head in my arms. Their final act of cruelty was to tear me away from his dead body. I lost the will to live. I wanted to end my life at once and join Alex. Why didn't they shoot me? Why did they allow me to live? Without hesitation, I ran towards the high tension wire fence. I thought ''I will just have to touch it before the guards catch up with me and that will be the end''. But as I reached the fence an elderly SS guard stood squarely in my way. ''Why do you want to die?'' he asked gently — the first gentle voice apart from Alex's that I had heard since I lost Aranka. ''You seem so young. The war will soon be over and it will be our turn to perish. I know you will live. Besides, look! Can't you see there is no current in the barbed wire fence — the red bulbs are not aglow!'' He then touched the fence with his bare hands to prove that it was not alive. The Third Reich was on the brink of collapse and this was an economy measure to save electricity! He looked around anxiously, in case the other guards would hear what he was telling me. That elderly German concentration camp guard was visibly upset by the sudden and tragic death of Alex Petrushka. For him too Alex had become a familiar figure, like a piece of furniture which belonged to the camp. Maybe he had listened to his music and had been moved by this wretched prisoner playing beautifully while he lived out an ugly and tormented existence. Perhaps he was moved to transfer this sympathy from the dead Alex to the shaven headed, skinny, but still living girl that cowered before him.

''Alex's guard'', as I came to think of him, was the only guard whose face I could remember in later years. Whether I had seen them in Budapest or in the German prison camps, they were all faces that one sees in a succession of mirrors at varying angles; dehumanised! Young or old, blond or dark, they all took the same form, like a set of toy soldiers, all with the same anonymous faces.

Again, one of the miracles in my life happened. Instead of being shot, I was merely ordered back to my wooden bunk prostrate with grief.

After Alex's death I felt numb and was in a totally dazed condition. For days and weeks I wandered around the camp doing my duties like a sleepwalker, every move and action an automatic reflex done without reason or feeling. There was nothing left for me to live for; life had no purpose or meaning. I felt that all my strength and hope of survival had vanished; for me, this must be the end of the road. It was not to be so. Life did not end, and I was to suffer a lot more later.

CHAPTER 4

Just Existence

My existence in the camp followed the same pattern — near starvation and hard labour every day without respite. We were being methodically reduced to skeletons. More and more of the inmates died every day and their bodies were shovelled into crude holes, without any kind of religious service. Diseases too were taking a large toll. Some inmates disappeared to a block set apart from the rest. Rumours spread, which were later confirmed, that these poor unfortunate people were incarcerated in so-called "medical wards" where the most gruesome inhuman experiments were performed. One day, much to our surprise, we were given pieces of soap. It seemed an incongruous gesture, as our guards allowed us scarcely enough water with which to wash ourselves. From this act, speculation and rumours grew, and the adults eventually realised that the soap was in fact made from the fat of human bodies. We were washing with the remains of our friends and loved ones. As a final gesture the remaining soap was buried in the earth and a prayer offered that their souls might rest in peace. An even deeper despair seemed to settle upon us in this poignant moment, and as a child I wondered why this was happening to me. What had I done and for what was I being punished? My happy carefree life had suddenly and inexplicable been snatched away from me, and I was now living in misery and desolation.

My mind drifted constantly to thoughts about my parents and my brother. At each arrival of a new batch of prisoners I would anxiously scan the faces of the rows and rows of men and women, looking for my dear father and mother, yet deep down hoping that they would not be amongst them. I hoped and prayed that they would be spared the fate I was now enduring. For some inexplicable reason, I never looked for my brother, for I just knew that he would not be there. I used to have a strange recurring dream about him. In my dream, there would be a revolving glass door — the kind one sees at the entrance to a hotel — and my brother would be trapped within this door, just going round and round, never stopping and never coming out. I did not understand the meaning of the dream, but I did know not to expect to see my brother in the camps.

My recollections of those days seem to have been blurred by the constant hardship and monotony. I think back to it now with a strange detachment — almost as if it had been an episode enacted by other people on another planet. It seems like an eternity ago; another time, another place, another me. "Feelings" and "emotions" were just words to be remembered. It was as though they had been put on ice, to be preserved for use at some later date. My memories are of darkness and doom; heaviness, depression, desolation — everything enveloped in a shroud of grey gloom. I have no recollections of colours or textures. I cannot remember spring or summertime, or seeing flowers and greenery. It is as though my finer senses went to sleep during that black period of my life and a lock placed on whatever might have awakened my mind and memory to beauty and delight. Yet despite this, despite the weakness of my body, something, somehow, helped me to survive those desperate years. God had given my spirit and I like to think that this together with my faith and trust in Him helped carry me through.

From time to time I would hear the grown-ups talking about the progress of the war. It seemed that Germany was in a sorry state, and that the guards at Dachau expected the allies to arrive at any time now. But would we survive long enough to be liberated? Our captors continued their programme of mental and physical torture with a sickening diligence which no doubt pleased their Fuhrer.

One day during the winter we were all called from our bunks, told to undress and made to stand naked in the freezing cold. We had to remain still for as long as we could endure the biting elements. Many people in their sick debilitated state were unable to survive this cruel exercise. Those who collapsed and died from exhaustion and exposure were at least spared further beating by the guards. The "kapos" or "trusties", chosen from the ranks of long-serving criminals, or sometimes Jews who the Germans had selected for their looks or promising strength, were often worse than the guards. Many had earned their privileged status by informing on their fellow inmates, or by treating the so-called "political prisoners" or Jews with extreme cruelty. One of the "rewards" was to be selected either by women guards as their lovers, or by the men to become camp prostitutes.

Most of the time I kept very much to myself, either shutting out all thoughts, or composing little stories in my mind about the daily incidents within the camp, anything to help pass the time during those endless days and nights. I would keep clear of any disturbances and be as unobtrusive as possible to the guards. That way I would stand a better chance of survival. However, on one occasion I did voice my opinion, despite the danger in doing so. I was returning from a "privileged" trip to the toilet, and as I hurried back to my barracks I saw close by a dark haired very lovely young woman. In those surroundings she looked outstandingly beautiful; pink cheeked, healthy and well-fed. She wore boots and a fur coat and was obviously a "kapo". As I was about to enter my section, she hit out at me with her truncheon and hurt and indignation welled up inside me. Without thinking of the consequence I cried out at her. "Why do you do this?" I demanded. "There is no-one watching you, no Germans to whom you must prove yourself or show off! You are Jewish yourself yet you beat innocent people. I am weak and starving, yet you want to beat me. Believe me, God will punish you". With each angry word, I realised my danger, yet I had to give vent to my feelings. Instead of beating me further she had the grace to blush deeply then she turned and walked away. From then on whenever she saw me she would avoid coming close. Young and frail as I was, I always believed that God had given me the strength and courage to speak to that kapo the way that I did.

During my imprisonment at Dachau some of the younger inmates including myself were selected to work on the land nearby. The neat Bavarian farmyard and the countryside made a welcome change from the perpetual stench of death and disease at the camp. We were allowed to sleep in the hay — a luxury which did not last long. After a strenuous day's work we were tired and hungry, and to starving humans the grain scattered on the earth for the chickens was a temptation. I and several others tried to pick up a few grains, cramming what we could into our mouths. The farmer's family spotted the attempted theft and lost no time in reporting the incident to the guards. The guards cursed us and screamed that we had disobeyed the rules and had to be punished. If we had actually eaten the precious poultry feed, we would undoubtably have been put to death. Instead we were merely beaten. One of the guards rushed over to me and with his rough hands scrapped out of my mouth the few grains I had managed to gather. He tore at my tender lips, damaging the flesh in his fury. The farmer and his family looked on, totally indifferent to our cries. Later I came to wonder at such disinterest in human suffering. The only explanation for their behaviour that I can offer is that they had absorbed completely the potent poison supplied by the Reich's efficient propaganda machine. They had been told that the inmates of the camps were enemies of the German people, or criminals opposed to the prosperity of their country. One wonders what dreadful crimes we children were purported to have committed.

Shortly after this incident Dachau was partially evacuated because of the Allied advance and we embarked on a series of forced marches which led nowhere.

It was about this time that I became aware of a young girl who attached herself to me. Although she was older than I — about 15 or 16 — she was very immature and I suspected, mentally subnormal. For the most part she was unobtrusive and seemed just to want to stay by me. I remember well her close cropped hair and the deep dark ringed eyes that seemed to dominate her bony face. Like everyone else she was dressed in rags, and round her thin body she clutched the shreds of a blanket. She spoke very little and was somewhat withdrawn. Most of the time she would be quiet and subdued, but at other times she would be overcome by hysterical sobbing. These emotional outbursts put everyone's life at risk, for the German soldiers would seize such opportunities to flog or shoot the culprits and anyone else who came within their line of fire. On these occasions everyone would try to calm and quieten her and I came to feel a measure of responsibility for this poor tormented girl. Just as in the past I had found someone stronger than myself to look to for help and comfort, so she looked now to me for companionship. Whether the horror of her present surroundings had affected her mind or whether she had always been mentally deranged I never knew, but I was glad to think that maybe I was of some comfort to her.

On one of our many gruelling marches, we were given a portion of bread. Each portion was like a miniature loaf, a coarse dark bread usually given to the soldiers. As we queued for our ration we were kicked and beaten, but still we waited for this little piece of luxury. The abuse hurled at us ironically contained some good advice, though it was not with good intentions that they screamed at us not to gobble it all at once like animals. We must make it last, for it was the only bread we would see for the next three weeks! Alas, many people did gobble it all at once, and in so doing added themselves to the ranks of the dead. Their skeleton bodies had been starved of food for so long that just one small loaf proved too much for their shrunken stomachs. Bloated and swollen they just keeled over and died.

The trek across the countryside continued as step by step we took the blows and abuse from the guards. My own strength was beginning to deteriorate rapidly and it was an effort to keep a grip on my remaining portion of bread. It was also becoming a mounting ordeal even to keep my shoes on. Sizes too big for my tiny feet, the only way I could walk in them was by curling my toes up in any effort to maintain a grip. To this day, my toes are deformed as a result. I was becoming so weak that the effort was proving too much, and I considered abandoning my shoes. Then I remembered how much I suffered from the cold, so with the help of a few torn-up rags bound around my feet I managed to hang on to my shoes.

I suddenly developed a craving for onion! The thought of biting into one filled my dreams day and night and no exotic food could at that time have given me more pleasure than a simple onion. I might just as well have been craving caviar for there was no hope of me finding one, although I was constantly on the lookout whenever we passed a village or farm. I remember hearing my parents talking about someone they knew who had been sent to prison. They were discussing his needs, and also the prison food, and I recall their saying that if someone could get onion or garlic to him, it would help him keep healthy as both were good for the lungs. Perhaps I was subconsciously remembering this incident when my craving began.

Our intervals of rest were brief, maybe an hour or two, when we were somtimes served a bowl of lukewarm rhubarb water. On odd occasions we would stop at a farm where we would be allowed to sleep in the hay. Here at least we could usually count on a few hours undisturbed rest. The interminable roll-calls and naked parades for counting were never carried out in front of civilians. Maybe the German soldiers had a conscience and did not want to offend the eyes of their compatriots. At one such farm where we stopped to rest one night, the dark eyed girl came and lay by my side in the hay, and we snuggled into its welcome warmth, weak and exhausted. Early next morning, just before daybreak we were roused to continue our trek. My companion was searching for something in the hay without success, and second by second her distress grew into a mounting frenzy. It seemed that she had somehow managed to save a piece of her bread, and as was the custom, had slept with it beneath her head so that it would not be stolen from her. Now she could not find it. She screamed accusations at everyone — including me — and became completely hysterical. A few people tried to muffle her cries and calm her, but they were too weak to be effective. In this frenzied state she was taken by the guards to be transferred to the hospital. We all knew what that meant. I shed tears for her, though I knew neither her name nor her number, and I was never to see her again. Later I asked after her whereabouts, and although several people knew of her going into hospital no-one ever heard of her coming out.

My young constitution had so far withstood the effects of starvation, frequent beatings and maltreatment, even typhus which had raged throughout the camp. It seemed that my spirit had overcome my physical state and was urging me not to give in. We hoped and we prayed that the end was near for our captors. The dying days of 1944 were cold and bitter, but we had faith that the Spring of 1945 would bring us freedom and life — if only we could survive that long. Rumours again abounded that the allied armies were sweeping ahead. We knew that it would only be a matter of time before they stumbled upon a death camp, and then the full truth and horror which earlier they had refused to believe would be revealed. Whether we would still be alive to welcome our liberators was another matter.

CHAPTER 5

Brief Respite

It seemed that we had been on the move sometimes on foot, sometimes by train for weeks on end. I began to think that we were lost. Maybe even our guards did not know our destination. Conditions were indescribable with total lack of hygiene or sanitation and very little food or water. At one point of our journey we seemed to be under constant air attack with bombs falling all around us and sometimes hitting the wagons. Many in other sections were killed, but somehow fate saved me from death at that time. Years later, I discovered that the bombing we suffered then, was part of an allied air offensive on Berlin. How we came to be there I do not know. Although I escaped the bombing I was in a state of near collapse. I was suffering from hunger and exposure from the open wagons, and my fingers were so frozen that I had lost all sense of feeling in them. I again saw many of my fellow-travellers die. Death had become so commonplace to me, yet I was still only 12 years old.

The word went round that we were to stop at a camp where conditions were good, where there was food and comfortable accommodation, and even a hospital. By this time I was well past caring. I felt that I had come to the end of my strength and could carry on no longer. However, one day we did arrive — on foot — at the so called "sample camp". I could not believe what I saw there. Just as in any normal hospital grounds there were beautifully laid-out flower beds surrounded by green, green, grass. Everything had a clean neat look about it and even the barracks looked pleasant. I saw people standing or working; the men cleanshaven, everyone dressed in clean clothing — old and worn perhaps — but nevertheless, tidy and presentable. My hopes leapt at the sight of these civilised conditions. Maybe the war had ended and this was our liberation! The splash of colour from the flower gardens delighted my childish mind. It was so artistic, so pretty. The whole aspect was so serene that it seemed to blot out the soldiers with their guns, the guard-dogs and the watch-towers. The place in which we found ourselves was in fact a "model camp", which the Red Cross officials were allowed to visit when they investigated the living and working conditions of the prisoners of the Reich. Not, of course a true representation of the concentration camps, but merely a "show-piece", cleverly constructed to appease the concern of the neutrals. Perhaps the adult prisoners realised this but it did not register on my young mind. To me it looked like heaven and I felt a surge of hope and new-found energy.

Signs of the camp's true nature remained however. Looking around I saw guards with their guns and ever-present truncheons and spotted someone on the ground being kicked. We entered the barracks where again I thought that my eyes were deceiving me. No long hard multi-beds here, but separate bunks with clean soft straw. It was sheer luxury! Before and after, I was never to see another camp like it. My surge of happiness was short-lived however. The bell summoned us to an interminable roll-call not ten minutes after our arrival. At any time, day or night, that dreaded bell would rouse us for inspection and counting. In all weathers, rain, gales or blizzards, we would be made to stand for hours on end until at last someone would come to count us. This could be repeated as often as took their fancy, and nearly every inspection would end with a number of inmates collapsing and dying through exhaustion and exposure. We would be sent back to our beds or to work, only to be subjected to a repeat performance a short time later.

At the end of our first roll-call in this "model" camp, we were told that we would be given hot soup and a slice of bread. The bread portion was small and dry but it was food, and food meant life. Some of the people did not have the strength even to queue. A young woman behind me dropped her tin cup and I stooped to pick it up and quickly pushed it back into her hands. Had I held it for her myself it would have looked as though I had two cups, and I would not have been allowed to keep it. It bothered me wondering if she would manage, but I soon forgot about her when I was given my ration of food. I gobbled the bread and drank the soup quickly so that I might regain my strength. We returned to the barracks and I sank wearily onto a bunk, into the clean, sweet-smelling straw. I revelled in its softness and warmth, savouring this wondrous luxury. My tired body drifted into that pre-sleep state of complete relaxation, only to be rudely roused minutes later for yet another inspection.

I awoke the next morning with a raging toothache. The pain was so great that I screamed out in agony. This I thought must be the end for me. To shout or create a disturbance in front of the guards was fatal but the pain was so excruciating that I could not contain my cries. I knew that the noise was endangering not only my own life but also that of my fellow-prisoners. When two guards rushed in guns at the ready shouting "What's happening? What is the noise about?", I knew that I would be shot. "She has toothache", someone answered in German, "and the pain is unbearable for her". My guardian angel must have been watching over me for instead of being marched out and shot, I was told I would be seen by the camp dentist! I could not believe it was true, but sure enough I was taken to the surgery. "Taken" is hardly the right word, for I was pushed and kicked all the way there. Even so, stumbling and falling, and all the time in agonizing pain from my tooth, we arrived at a building marked "hospital". Red Cross flags fluttered nearby, and I thought that maybe I was going to be used for experimentation. I hesitated at the door but was helped inside by the boot of one of my guards. Inside the hospital by the dentist's surgery stood a healthy good-looking young Jewish doctor dressed in a spotless white coat. By his side was a beautiful German nurse, also wearing a white coat underneath which I could see the insignia of the SS. The doctor extracted my tooth with practiced gentle hands, explaining that he was unable to give me a pain-killing injection as none was available. After the extraction he gave me a pill, and I must admit that it freed me from the pain of the toothache. I found it incredible that I had been allowed medical attention instead of being shot or beaten to death. The soldiers escorted me back to the barracks. I was not spared their blows and kicks, but after the pain I had suffered from the toothache their punishment was bearable — and I was still alive.

This short episode in my life ended the following day when we left our "model" prison. As we were herded together ready to move out, I saw other prisoners approaching, no doubt looking forward as we had done to rest, food and shelter. The dream was over, and the nightmare was to continue.

CHAPTER 6

Shot

On and on we tramped and travelled. On foot and by train, alternating one with the other. For how long or where to, no-one knew. I moved and reacted like a robot. "Walk!", I walked "Stop!, I stopped. It was as though my body was responding but my soul was in limbo. We dragged ourselves on, hardly ever stopping for rest, and by now completely without supplies of food. Our only nourishment was from what we could find growing in the earth. We ate grass, roots, berries, leaves — anything to stop the gnawing hunger pains which were our constant companions. I remember eating roots from what looked to me like a Christmas tree. Perhaps we even ate parts of plants which were poisonous, but we neither knew nor cared. We were going to die anyway. Maybe poison was a blessing in disguise.

Where my stamina to continue came from I shall never know, but eventually my strength gave out, and I collapsed from weakness and exhaustion. Amazingly, I was not trampled on and crushed to death by the endless marching feet, nor did the guards notice my collapse. How long I lay there I do not know, but as I struggled to stand up I could not for the moment remember where I was. Then I saw the corpse-like figures ahead of me and the living nightmare flooded back into my brain. As I tried to catch up with the group, one of the guards spotted me and must have realised that I could walk no further. "Go over to the trees little one", he said "rest awhile, and when you see the tail-end of the group you can join us again". His voice was soft and gentle and I just did as he said, as though I was in a trance. Dazed, I crawled over to the roadside where I stumbled and fell. I turned to look at the guard and saw his automatic pointing at me. Numbly I stared at it. So this was to be the end. I had no will or energy to run away, and I just waited for the end to come. I heard the shots from his gun, felt a great pain in my leg and lost consciousness.

I lay there by the roadside drifting in and out of consciousness, unaware of the length of time that passed. An hour, a day, two days? I kept hearing the voice of the German guard saying "Rest, little one", and I could see his uniformed body and rounded helmet but no face. Everything was hazy and his voice was like an echo in a long, dark tunnel. I struggled to clear my mind and to drag myself out of the thick fog which seemed to envelope me. Was I dead? Had I dreamed about the guard pointing his gun at me and shooting? I touched myself and realised that I was feeling intense pain. I gradually focused my aching eyes, and through the haze saw a group of prisoners marching towards me. Was it "my" group? From the sounds and snatches of sentences I heard I realised that they were French prisoners. I knew very little French but understood the gist of the conversation when they spotted me. The French soldiers wanted to pick me up and help me but the German guard wanted to leave me for the next consignment of Jews who would pass and could take me with them. The French appeared to insist, and the guard, perhaps not wishing to appear too callous in front of fellow soldiers who still retained their code of honour, allowed them to retrieve my body. I vaguely remember being carried into some kind of Red Cross ambulance and hearing a voice say "sorry" before splashing me with alcohol and gouging out the bullets from my leg. There was no painkiller, and I can remember feeling the knife, but mercifully I was drifting in a semi-conscious state. A branch from a tree provided a splint and my legs were bound with rags. Later I was told that the doctor who had performed the make-shift operation was, like myself, Hungarian. I remember his gentleness as he tended me when I drifted back to awareness, and I noticed his worn ragged clothing. His was one of the few faces that I could bring to mind in later years. I was in great pain, delirious, and like a little skeleton, just another of the ghosts with whom I had marched. I remained in the ambulance, slipping in and out of consciousness until one day I awoke to find myself in another concentration camp. My new home was Bergen-Belsen.

Belsen concentration camp. To those who survived it the name brings back memories of horrific existence, to those who liberated it pictures of indescribable suffering.

My first recollections of the camp were hazy as I was very weak, in great pain and unable to walk properly on account of my injured leg. As I gained strength and became aware of my surroundings I saw that everything and everyone seemed to be completely disorganised. Neither the guards nor the prisoners seemed to know just what was happening. About the camp grounds corpses and clothing were being burnt on bonfires and the stench was beyond description. As I hopped and limped about the sights were so horrific that I do not think my child's mind was able to grasp the significance of what I was witnessing. Although I remember the suffering and the misery as though it were yesterday, at that time the full horror did not properly register with me. Corpses were rounded up daily and transported to the pits or the fires which the prisoners themselves had to dig or stoke. How many of the inmates had to dispose of their own loved ones and friends? How many mothers, fathers and children had been shovelled into those unconsecrated resting places? How many minds were permanently damaged and hearts broken by the horror of it all? The "Master Race" was doing its job well. For so many Jews, Belsen was the end of the line.

My own survival instinct made me remember some of Alex Petrushka's advice. To find out where the kitchens were in the hope of maybe finding and stealing some food. Avoiding the guards, who seemed not to be taking too much notice anyway, I hopped and hobbled around looking for the kitchens. I cannot recall where or how I found it, but somehow I retrieved a small potato. What a prize! I hopped over to one of the burning fires and dropped my potato into its embers to cook. The smell from the charred remains of clothes and who-knows-what else was appalling, but starvation makes a person none too particular, and at that moment all I could think of was food. I sat down near the fire watching my potato and saw many pairs of eyes, sunk deeply into hollow faces, looking at me in hopeful anticipation. I turned, and saw walking towards me a very beautiful SS woman. Tall, blue-eyed and blonde, she had an attractive figure, lovely even teeth, and — I noticed — a pair of expensive-looking boots. In later years I was told that she was the famous Irma Grace, but as seventy per cent of the female guards looked like her, she could have been anyone. Smiling, she approached me. "It's nice to warm your hands by the fire, isn't it?", she asked softly. Then her expression changed. She pushed me closer to the fire, ordered me to cover the potato with my hand, and with her heavy jackboot stamped on it and ground my fingers into the fire, crushing the still-hard potato beneath my hand. The pain was unbearable, the bones in my hand were crushed, and I bore the scars from the burns for years to come.

Listening to the inmates and witnessing the attitudes of the guards, it seemed to us that Germany was close to downfall. Our captors no longer shot people on sight, the watchtowers and searchlights were no longer manned twenty four hours a day, and many of the guards went about the camps unarmed. The bonfires however continued to burn, probably to dispose of evidence before the allies arrived. I am convinced that many of the bodies heaped onto the piles to await cremation still had life, though only just. Maybe they had collapsed from starvation and had been collected from the ground as though they were dead. This is how I was found when the allies marched into Belsen. On top of a heap of corpses, awaiting my final resting place — the funeral pyre.

CHAPTER 7

Liberation

"To be, or not to be", that was the awesome question when the allies arrived at Belsen concentration camp. To be alive, or not to be alive; which was better? I had already been counted as dead and thrown upon a pile of bodies. I was just conscious but unable to move. A haze of impressions flitted through my mind as I lay there. The potato and the fire, the smile on the SS woman's beautiful face, the endless train journeys and the forced marches, Aranka, Alex Petrushka, my parents. Everything swam before me like a moving montage.

The allied forces had arrived and we were free! In my dazed condition I watched as the inmates charged the store house where the food was kept and ransacked the building. For many it was their death sentence. After months of starvation their stomachs were unable to cope with the amount of food they frenziedly stuffed into their frail bodies. Having survived the atrocities inflicted by their captors they finally killed themselves in a frenzy of eating. To the well-fed intelligent person it is common logic that a starved body must be reintroduced to food gradually. To a body dying for want of nourishment, food of any kind the more the better, means life. In fact, it meant death to so many of my fellow inmates. Next, they had raided the clothing warehouse. They cast off their pitiful flea-infested rags exchanging them for the garments which had been taken from them. Fine underwear, warm dresses and trousers, coats and furs, all were seized. Within minutes every mink, Persian lamb and other fur coat had an owner. But how cruel fate can be. In touching what was rightfully theirs, they lost the chance of retaining their restored possessions. Our liberators commandeered the lot. Typhoid and cholera were rife amongst the inmates and everything and everybody was infested with fleas and lice. To safe-guard spreading disease the Allies had no alternative but to burn everything. At first nobody could understand why. Were we still to be denied our possessions? Once again everyone was forced to surrender the clothes they were wearing. It was logical, but logic played no part in our lives in Belsen.

For the Germans it was the end; for some of the inmates too, as the kapos were lynched by those they had so mercilessly kicked and beaten. Among the rest of the inmates many were too sick in mind and body to realise just what was happening and were unaware that their day of liberation had arrived.

I was drifting through a dense fog. My eyes flickered open and shut as I tried to think where I was. Was I dead? I did not think so. I moved my head and tried to look around me. I heard voices in many languages speaking softly close by. I wondered whether I was dreaming. As my eyes focused properly I saw nurses and doctors and beds with clean white sheets. The room was long, like a barrack room, and the patients in the beds around me were all like skeletons. As I moved my head several doctors and nurses came towards me. They spoke to me gently in several languages, and when they realised that I understood German and English, started asking me questions. The events of the last few days came back to me as I lay in my clean, fresh, comfortable bed. I remembered the men with their white armbands, the arrival of the allies and the raids upon the storehouses. But what was I doing here? Who were these people, these doctors and nurses? Suddenly I realised. I knew. They were going to use me for some unspeakable experiment. I became hysterical, screaming that I would rather die, I didn't want to be part of their terrible experiments. Somehow, they managed to calm me down and convince me that I was being taken care of in a real hospital where there were no more German guards. Finally, I realised that I was in safe hands.

From all over the world they came; doctors and nurses anxious to help the victims who had survived the living hell of Belsen. I was questioned about what had happened. How had I received my wounds? How did my hand come to be crushed and burnt? It was explained to me that my leg had been put in plaster to help it mend, but that later, I would probably need to have an operation. It would be scarred and ugly to look at, but I would soon be able to walk on it again. I answered what questions I could and gave an account of what had happened to me. Looking around the rest of the corpse-like bodies, their ribs sticking through their pitiful paper-thin flesh, skin peeling from their faces, I wondered if I looked the same as they, and I asked for a mirror. I was told that I had lost my hair as a result of typhoid fever, and that when my hair began to grow again, then I could have a mirror to see myself. Slowly, gradually, with care and attention, I gained strength and made progress. Perhaps because youth is more resilient and I progressed quicker than the rest, I was soon known as the 'miracle child'' — the youngest patient in the hospital. Every visitor to the hospital was brought to see me, and my facility with languages allowed me to be of use to the staff by interpreting their conversations with patients and visitors. I was spoiled by everyone, and I was showered with little gifts, extra food and a great deal of attention. I appreciated the kindness I was shown but I began to wonder about my own dear parents and brother. Were they still alive and looking for me, and would I ever see them again?

One day while still in hospital an important visitor was brought to see me. He was the town Major of

Hanover — Major Tommy Chutter. He came to visit on several occasions doing all he could to help those who had suffered so abominably. He always came to talk to me and one day asked me a question which was to have great bearing on my immediate future — would I be willing for him to adopt me? I asked him to give me time to think it over. The following day Major Chutter returned with friends and I decided to accept his proposal. I was now clear of infection so I was allowed to leave the hospital. My foot was still in plaster, but I was able to walk on it. I made only one stipulation: I refused to be treated by a German doctor. The memories were too vivid and I had an understandable fear and mistrust of German medical staff. There were obviously German doctors and nurses who were daily saving lives and tending to the sick, but my young mind was still suspicious and fearful. The only Germans I might have trusted were the nuns. My father had always told me that those who wore the uniform of God, whatever their religion Jew or Gentile, were to be trusted. So my wish was respected, and I was never treated by a German doctor or nurse. For a long time, even the sound of German voices made me nervous, even when I was free and living in Hanover.

In the care of Major Chutter I met many different people; high ranking officers, doctors, Red Cross workers, all kind and very friendly, who made me feel at ease. The Major did his utmost to help all the refugees from Bergen-Belsen who came to him seeking work and help. In my case, probably because I was so young, the care and attention was extra special. So that I might remain in his care, the Major had to put me on file as being part of the work force at the local Hanomac factory. When I was stronger and more mobile, I went to the factory to do my share of work. Filing was the first job I was given, but having had no previous experience at this or any other work, my efforts left much to be desired. In despair the man in charge asked Major Chutter to take me away. "I will keep her name on the records file", he said, "but do me a favour and take her back". So, home I went!

"Home" was a very pleasant villa which I shared with a few other girls, each having her own room. A handful of officers were assigned to us, to take us out, entertain us and generally ensure our wellbeing. An officer called Geoffrey took care of me, and his charm and attention were of great help and comfort during that period of physical recuperation and mental adjustment. What a sight I must have looked! I think he must have taken pity on the little waif he was assigned to. Much later, he told me how I had looked in those first days when no-one would allow me to have a mirror. An emaciated, frail little figure, skin yellowed and peeling, with a fuzz of hair just beginning to sprout again. That was Geoffrey's first impression of me! The officers took us swimming, to concerts, anywhere where we could learn to adjust to a normal way of living and gain some pleasure out of life. Geoffrey seemed to spend more time with me than with the other girls, and I came to depend on him very much. I looked upon him like an older brother, and a special bond developed between us which has lasted through the years. Today, I am still in contact with him and his lovely family, and I shall never forget his kindness and consideration during that difficult time.

The Major's wife, Clover, came to visit one day, and I was brought to meet her. We talked about the possibility of adoption, and afterwards she used to write me the most beautiful letters, expressing the wish that one day I might become her adopted daughter. Uppermost in my mind was the constant question of whether or not my parents were still alive. I had a deep feeling that they were, and Major Chutter did all within his power to trace them. He used the field post to make enquiries, but communications were still slow and intermittent.

In those early weeks after the liberation, time seemed to pass by very quickly. After the misery and tedium of months in a concentration camp life had suddenly become interesting and exciting again. The one thing that I did become sensitive about though, was my lack of clothes. The other girls seemed always to have something different to wear, while I had only my one sailcloth dress. How, I wondered, did they come to have such a variety? Shyly, I mentioned it to Major Chutter, who at the time was at a loss for an answer. However, soon afterwards, we found out. It appeared that the girls had found German dressmakers, and in exchange for their cigarette and egg-powder rations, were able to afford new clothes. I had never been given a cigarette ration — maybe the girls had thought me too young, and had kept my allowance for themselves. That, however, was soon rectified, and one day the major brough me some curtain material and took me to a dressmaker. "Little girl" he said, "here is some nice material. Have a couple of dresses made out of it. You are only small, it won't take much". So, I designed my first dress. I wanted a pinafore style, so that I could wear different blouses underneath, and I had my dresses made with my curtain material, paying for them with my egg powder and cigarette rations.

Our villa still had all the furniture and belongings of its German owners, including their clothes. At any time, I could have worn something from the clothes they had left, but I remembered my father's teaching — never to take that which did not belong to you. We had all been warned that should the owners return asking for their possessions, we were to refuse them entry. One day when I was alone and the girls were all at work, I answered a knock on the door. A middle-aged man stood there, anxiety showing on his face. He said the house was his, and that, although he knew that he was forbidden to enter, could I possibly let him have some of his sheets for his family as he could not afford to replace them. He looked genuinely upset, and I hesitated before deciding what to do. My decision was impetuous and foolish but I told him to come in and help himself. I never revealed this incident to anyone, and was afterwards always slightly ill at ease when alone in the house. He came once more, and again I let him in and told him to take whatever he wanted. Maybe I should not have taken pity on him the way I did. After all when the soldiers left, his home and possessions were returned to him, unlike the Jews whose homes had been looted and permanently confiscated or destroyed.

Despite my new clothes, I still felt a bit like the ugly duckling. When the other girls went out to parties, I invariably stayed home, alone. The one other person who always made my feel welcome was one of the Major's secretaries. She was a very attractive lady, who travelled everywhere with him on business. They were always given the "Red Carpet" treatment, and whenever possible, I would go with them, riding along in the jeep like a little mascot. She was a little older than I, and very kind to me. We are still firm friends today.

Several months passed as I adjusted to my new life. I was as happy as the circumstances would allow, then something happened to make my happiness complete. Information had arrived about my parents. They were alive! They had spent many anxious months trying to trace me, and had almost given up hope, but eventually they had received my letters through the field post.

I was ecstatic with joy, but the joy was marred by the information that my brother was dead, shot by the Danube not long after he had left home that second time. The news was given to me by the Major, who undoubtedly had mixed feelings. He was pleased for me that I had traced my parents, but sad that I would not now become his adopted daughter.

Next door to our villa lived more refugee girls, and from time to time I would drop in to see them and pass some time. I was there one day when a very beautiful lady arrived, accompanied by her two small nieces. She called herself "Baroness Thyssen". She was blonde, elegantly dressed, and wore lots of diamonds. The girls who lived in that house knew her as "Ily" and also as "the Baroness". Even the officers referred to her as "Baroness Thyssen". She disapproved of my "dropping in" and getting under her feet, and let me know it, although she was quite kind to me and gracious. One day, I saw much coming and going of British Officers, and the next day she was gone and I never found out what happened to her.

As I gained strength I did eventually start work, and I began to make preparations to meet my father in Prague. The waiting extended into weeks, then months, for travel was still not easy, and the Major wanted to ensure that my journey would be comfortable and safe. My father however could not wait in Prague any longer. He had to return with my mother to Hungary to continue his work, so he left a message and instructions with the Red Cross, saying he would meet me in Prague when I could at last make the journey.

Major Chutter promised me that when I left for Prague he would give me a parcel of food to take with me, for food was extremely scarce throughout Europe. The day of my departure dawned. I gathered together my few possessions, a couple of pictures, my clothing and the food parcel. Our goodbyes were filled with poignant memories. My benefactor looked fondly at me, the once bald little waif he had nearly adopted. The ugly duckling was finally going home.

My route involved changing trains many times. The journey was protracted by long waits for trains which never arrived. The carriages were filled with soldiers heading for various destinations. One night, when I was sleeping, my small canvas bag was stolen from me. Everything I had in the world was in that bag. Pictures, Alex Petrushka's amulet, and the food from Major Chutter. I cried bitterly. I think everyone felt sorry for me when they saw me crying, but no amount of searching found my bag. Once again, I had lost all my possessions.

CHAPTER 8

Reunion

Major Chutter had written to my father telling him to expect my arrival in Prague in three weeks time. Because of the infrequency and unreliability of the trains, it was impossible to stipulate the exact date, let alone the hour of arrival so my father had travelled to Prague expecting to wait maybe two or three days for me. After a week of anxious enquiries, of reading the notice boards at all the arrival points and meeting every train at the station, my father could wait no longer. Sad and dejected he returned to my mother in Budapest — alone.

When I eventually arrived in Prague, I found my father's anxious messages everywhere. At each arrival centre there were instructions from him of what to do and who to contact. He had stayed at what used to be the leading private hotel in Prague, and had known the wife of the former owner, a Jewish girl from the same suburb as my father. It seems that there were still one or two of the old employees working there, for my father had entrusted one of the porters with notes and some money for me. I had the choice of staying either at the hotel or at a transit place for people like myself. I decided to go to the transit centre. It looked as though in earlier days it might have been a hotel or large boarding house. Here problems arose as I did not possess identity papers so legally I had no existence! However, the identification which Major Chutter had provided me proved acceptable, I was given a set of clean clothes, food and a bed, and I settled down to await the arrival of my father. As he had instructed, I made a telephone call to Budapest from one of the Red Cross Aid centres, leaving a message for my father to say that I had arrived. This in itself was quite an operation. Back in Hanover I had always relied on the Major or one of his aides to do things for me; here I was on my own and had to act on my own initiative.

I rested and made the acquaitance of my neighbours who, like me, were all awaiting reunion with their family and friends. Everyone seemed to be plagued by the same weariness and mental fatigue. One day as I was resting on my bed wondering how long it would take for my father to arrive, I glanced towards the doorway just as the figure of a man entered the room. My heart started skipping beats and I held my breath. It was him. I felt faint, as if all my energy had suddenly drained from my body. I wanted to shout out to him and tell him that I was here, his little Agnes was waiting for him! I wanted everyone to know that he had come for me, that this man was my father and he had really come for me. But I could not move. I was paralysed. It was as though my body had become moulded to the bed. My lips were moving, but no sound came out. He looked the way I had always pictured him; in the concentration camps, through the period in Hanover, during the train journey to Prague, last week, yesterday, today, now! This neatly dressed man looking anxiously around, his dear face made older than his years by the worry lines etched by the war, this little white-haired, blue-eyed man was my father. I felt the hot tears stinging my eyes, and then the lump in my throat seemed to burst. I heard a voice scream out "Daddy!" — and realised that the voice was mine. It echoed through the room, and it was as though time, life, sound and motion had all stopped. Stumbling past furniture and startled faces I ran towards him. Racked by hysterical sobs we clung to each other, joy and misery overlapping and engulfing us in a sea of tears. I rested my head on his chest with my arms entwined fiercely round his waist. Over and over again I sobbed "Daddy, Daddy", while he kissed and stroked my hair, my face, my hands, soothing me and calming me down. I looked into his blue eyes brimming with tears, mirrors of my own unspoken feelings. The room was hushed, everyone's attention had focused on us, and many faces were wet with tears of compassion. Drained of pent up tension, we went to my little bed and sat down. My father told me about what had happened to him and my mother after losing me and my dear brother. They had carried on an existence, but the spirit had been taken from them. They went through the motions of life, but they were not living. Their lives were meaningless. My father's position had saved them from deportation, but life was hard, and in order to exist they had had to sell practically everything they owned. He told me about the plans he had made for me, and the school which I would attend. It was a special school for children like myself, who, because of the war, had missed out on their education. Situated here in Prague its aim was to fill in the gaps in our knowledge by intensive cramming.

After a little while he took me to the hotel where he was staying and made arrangements for our journey to Budapest. Before we left, he took me to meet the family with whom he had arranged I should stay during my year as a student. They seemed a nice enough family, the house was clean, modern and very close to the school, but I felt a coolness in their attitude towards me. I said nothing to my father, but I felt instinctively that I would not be happy there.

The journey to Budapest was no less complicated than the one from Hanover to Prague. I thought about my mother and the suffering she had endured, of how the onset of the Nazi regime with its restrictions, Jew baiting and ultimate atrocities had affected her personality. Even while I was still at home she had lost the ability to smile. I remembered her as being very serious, whereas my father had always tried to make my brother and I laugh, and provide some form of fun. I considered what had caused the change in my mother. Our house had been a refuge for all sorts of people, awaiting false "Aryan" papers. Although my father had made it a firm rule never to tell my mother what he was doing, lest she be questioned by the police, she was naturally under great strain. Just being a Jew was a strain; not allowed to have food rations, not allowed to live a normal life. Not knowing from one minute to the next whether you would be taken for interrogation, beaten or even killed. Then the shock of losing both children, one shot dead, the other gone without trace. I wondered what was going through her mind now as she awaited our arrival. My father had told her to wait for us at home, for with the state of the railway timetables, it was impossible to tell on which day we would arrive, but I knew that she would be at the station. What mother would not want to be there to meet a daughter she had thought dead? Anticipating another highly emotional scene, I began to prepare myself for our reunion. As I pondered the heartbreaks my parents had endured, my own problems seemed to diminish. I thought about my relatives and friends who had lost their loved ones, some still not knowing if they were alive or dead, shot or burned in Germany's great ovens or adrift amongst the mass of refugees. Each would have their own private hell, and reparation — if it were possible — would take a long time. As I mentally adjusted myself to the prospect of seeing my mother again, my spirits were high, and I grew excited as the train drew near to Budapest. My father tried to curb my excitement, telling me again that he had told my mother to wait for us at home. As we stepped down onto the platform, my father took charge of our few belongings as I eagerly scanned the faces of the waiting crowds. Suddenly I heard someone call out my nickname, and I saw my dear mother running towards us. Despite my self-discipline, my reaction was one of deepfelt emotion. Our reunion was heavily charged with feelings of happiness mixed with a sense of loss and deep grief. We embraced and clung to each other, weeping loud and long, letting the heartaches and the memories pour out with our tears. I mourned the loss of my dear brother; my mother the murder of her only son and first-born child. All the pent-up emotion which for so long had been repressed, albeit just below the surface, was now released in this moment of our meeting. As our sobs subsided and gave way to feelings of relief, we questioned each other about the events past and present. Sitting in the taxi going home, we talked about our friends and relatives who had survived. What had become of them! How many — or how few — were left? She told me of people who before the war had lived a good, comfortable, middle class life and who now existed in drastically reduced circumstances. Everything they had owned had been looted, destroyed or confiscated. Life was hard, food was scarce and the memories were still nightmares. It was unsafe to walk the streets wearing good clothes or carrying anything of value for fear of being robbed. My father had had an experience, amusing in the telling, but frightening and embarrassing in reality. One day, just a few hours after he had left for work, mother heard the doorbell ring. Looking through the peep-hole, she was amazed to see the figure of my father, barefoot and barelegged, clutching around him a railwayman's overcoat. So comical was the sight, she collapsed into helpless laughter, unable to open the door, much to the annoyance of my poor father who was standing there shivering! Apparently he had been on the train travelling to work when a man entered his compartment and forced him to remove and hand over his shoes and clothing. He was spared the embarrassment of total nudity by borrowing the railwayman's overcoat in which he returned home. Although my mother was overcome by hysterical laughter at the sight of my father, she was greatly relieved to discover that at least he had been spared physical violence. Many less fortunate had not.

There was a lovely meal waiting for us when we arrived at our flat, and I relished the taste of my mother's cooking. Friends and neighbours kept popping in to welcome me home; some I remembered, some I had been to school with, some had changed so much I did not recognise them, but the atmosphere generated was one of warmth and welcome. Before the war our home had been filled with fine furniture and paintings. Now the walls were bare and the rooms sparsely furnished. My father had been a good provider, often arriving home with a painting or piece of furniture to enhance the home. In particular I remembered a chair he had bought, which used to be in the hallway, and was a favourite of mine. It was wide and impressive, hand carved and fashioned apparently by the master craftsman who had made furniture for the Hapsburg family in Vienna. This too had gone. Despite the lack of material things, our home that day was a happy one. There was a family unity bonded by a love made deeper and more precious by the tragedies we had endured. That night as I lay in my bed, I felt a peace and comfort I had almost forgotten. My own room, and my dear mother and father close by. I closed my eyes and nestled into the soft blankets. I was at peace with the world.

I stayed with my parents longer than originally intended, and consequently missed the start of a new term at school. I was secretly quite relieved at not having to return to Prague as planned. I had not been looking forward to living with the family to whom I had been introduced. Instead, I met up with old friends, made a few new ones, and began to fit in to a normal kind of family life. Everyone was trying very hard to blot out the past, bury the memories and start a new life. It was customary in those days for the men to meet their friends early in the morning at a coffee house and discuss news and views over breakfast or coffee before going their respective ways to work. My father used to stop at one such place where there was a waiter who always paid him special attention. He seemed to have a certain respect and admiration for my father which did not pass unnoticed. My father was a man who liked a little flattery, and of this trait I am sure my mother was well aware! She too began to meet up with friends from the past, people who had really tried to help during the bad times, often putting themselves at risk. Gradually Budapest stirred back to life. We went to theatres and concerts, losing ourselves and our thoughts in the gaiety of the moment. Although the grand style of pre-war days, when everyone dressed up for the theatre, was missing, we dressed as best as we could, enjoying the resurgence of culture and entertainment. Old and young, we all joined together to make a new social life for ourselves. Laughter returned to our homes and on the streets and we no longer walked in fear or submission. Sometimes I would sense a moment of happiness when I saw mother laughing, seemingly free from the pain and heartaches she had endured. Then I would see her eyes of sadness which always betrayed her true feeling. She once told me that no matter what joys she might experience, no matter how much time went by, not a day of her life passed by without her feeling she would break her heart yet again over the loss of my brother. No matter in what circumstances death occurred, she said, one never forgot one's child, but to have your child murdered as her son was murdered, left a pain which could never be relieved.

For my own part, I was trying to adjust to my new life. At fourteen, I felt much older than my years, and my experiences had made me that much more mature. I became very friendly with a boy I had known at school when I was much younger, and we began to see a lot of each other. He was non-Jewish and came from a very nice family, but I think my parents became anxious lest I became too involved with him. My father had never been biased against non-Jews, in fact, he had helped many escape death during his wartime activities, but he did have understandably deep feelings about what he wanted for his only child. After all I had suffered for the very fact of being a Jew and he did not want me to become romantically attached to anyone not of our faith. Besides, I was too young to get involved in anything serious, and I still had to complete my education. I think my parents were both quite happy when the time came for me to return to Prague to continue my schooling. We found a very nice elderly couple for me to stay with. My room was clean and pretty with frilled curtains, a huge bed and a table covered with an embroidered cloth. I grew quite fond of the old lady who was unfortunately often in poor health. It was intended that I should complete a course in one term, then return to Budapest for a vacation with my parents, returning later to finish my education. The courses were run on a continuous basis so that students could join at whatever time was suitable to them, returning perhaps a year later to complete their studies. I was hungry for knowledge and eager to make up for lost time. Crash courses had been designed in mathematics, science, history and literature. Denied a normal education, it seemed I could not devour quickly enough the feast of learning now set before me. With youthful impatience I wanted everything to happen at once, but my past experiences had taught me that all things take time. With so much to think about, so much studying to do, the time raced by and the weeks turned into months. I was also becoming more aware of human attitudes and was growing proudly conscious of my Jewish identity. My experiences at the hands of the Nazis had made me a sensitive woman. I felt deeply when friends I had known before the Nazi occupation no longer wished to talk to me. Was it guilt or antisemitic indoctrination which made them avoid me? As a consequence I did not have many close friends with whom I could go out, so my evenings were mostly spent alone, studying. I remember that winter as being a cold hard one, with little social activity to relieve the dark evenings.

Like most young girls, I had hopes and dreams for the future, and my own dream was that I might meet someone with whom I could share my time and my thoughts; someone to talk to and laugh with and trust in. I did not actively seek out such a person, but always I had faith that one day I would meet someone special.

CHAPTER 9

Prague Encounter

One day, as I was leaving school I stopped in the street, hesitating for a moment over which direction to take. Not wishing to return immediately to my little room, I thought that I might look around awhile. Prague had been such a beautiful city — The Golden Prague — as it used to be called. I had visited the city in the past and had viewed its splendid architecture, felt its atmosphere and haunting beauty. I surveyed my surroundings with mixed emotions, as I thought about the circumstances which had brought me here. It was in this confused moment that I met Oldo, a young Czech medical student whom I had seen fleetingly from time to time. Descending the stairs behind me had had apparently noticed my hesitation. He greeted me, and with exquisite politeness offered his help. He was a slight figure with dark blond hair, thin lips, perfectly formed teeth, and the most striking blue-green eyes I had ever looked into. They were eyes which noticed everything, and now they were observing me. Something about his face drew me to him; some magic that emanated from those incredible eyes told me that he was somehow different and that it would be safe to accept his offer. In a second, this handsome young Czech had won me. I, who was normally so independent and self-sufficient, gladly accepted his services as my guide. Oldo was a true patriot; proud of his homeland and of Prague. We talked about the beauty of the city and he took me to see the old synagogue where the legend of Golem had originated. It was now sunk deep into the earth with age. We walked and we talked. Oldo told me about the history of Prague, about its buildings, its monuments and its people. I fell under the spell of Prague and was spellbound by Oldo himself. As we wandered through the main roads, the side streets and the little winding alleys, we talked about the past and the present, without mentioning the horrors of the Nazi occupation as if by some tacit agreement. On this unspoken understanding, I based my feelings that he knew that I was Jewish, but I was not really quite sure.

As evening fell and it became cooler, he took off his coat and wrapped it around me. I felt a warmth and affection for him, this young man whom I had only just met, but who I seemed to have known for ever and ever. His charm and sincerity enveloped me. Here was a man of culture, of good breeding. Wealth was not important to me — although by his clothes and wellgroomed appearance it was apparent that he was not impoverished — but background mattered to me very much. As a teenage girl I had dreams of being escorted by a young man whom I could admire, respect and look up to. After years of torment and mental torture it seemed that at last I was to experience the happiness for which I had yearned. When he took me in his arms and I looked into his eyes, I felt a magic I had never before known. Like a bottle of champagne I was filled with an effervescence bursting to be free. Free to love, free to live life so long denied to me.

We sat for a while on the bank of the River Moldava under the floodlit Hradzin. This was the castle which dominated the city, and even now stood like a bold sentry on guard. It was like a dream. He put his arm around me, protectively, and I felt completely and utterly happy. He spoke of his family who immediately came to life in my mind, of his ambitions, his country, and I in turn, told him about myself and my family. I spoke very little of the persecutions to which we had been subjected, and did not go into much detail about the concentration camps. He knew that I had been there, but then so had millions of others, Jew and Gentile alike. The reasons for incarceration were so many, but at that time neither of us felt the need to discuss them. We wished to speak of pleasant things, of beauty and of happiness. We understood each others thoughts as though we had known them since time began.

As evening became night he asked if I would like to eat. He took me to a small restaurant, and in his quiet, charming manner told me to order whatever I desired. I did not know whether or not he had money, but not wishing to take advantage of his generosity I chose something simple. When he saw what I had selected, he remarked on the modesty of my choice, but I was content just to eat and be with this charming young man.

As we left the restaurant it began to rain. Oldo hailed a taxi and took me home. Before kissing me gently goodnight, he asked me to meet him again, and we agreed to go out together the following Saturday evening. We could not meet sooner because I had to study for my end-of-term exams, and also my dear father was due to arrive the following day. He wanted to take me back with him to Budapest, knowing that I had progressed in my studies during my year's stay. At a later date I could return to Prague to continue them. I was, after all, his only surviving child, so it was natural for him to want me to be with him and my dear mother.

My father arrived and we stayed at the Alcron, the leading hotel in Prague. It was a wonderful, if somewhat emotional reunion. It was some time since I had seen my parents and the meeting brought back all the memories from the past. My father was bitterly disappointed when I told him that I wanted to stay in Prague. There were too many memories of fear and humiliation back in Budapest. The shock of sudden deportation at the age of eleven, the horrors of the forced march to the Austrian frontier; these were the things I could not forget. Besides, I was happy in Prague. I liked my school, enjoyed my studies, and had intended staying for another year to complete my courses, taking a holiday in between. Of course, now I had another reason for wanting to stay; I had met Oldo. I begged my father to let me stay for one more year. I felt I could not return to Budapest and face one-time friends and neighbours who had stood by and watched indifferently as the Nazis tore my family apart. I would be unable to settle back into a place of such bitter memories. My father was a true Hungarian; I was born in Czechoslovakia and felt at home in Prague. I felt guilty at not wanting to return with my father. I knew how much my parents wanted me to be with them, especially after the heart-breaking separation we had experienced, but deep inside me I felt I could be happy only if I stayed in Prague — and with my Oldo.

I lost no time in presenting Oldo to my father, and on Saturday night, as arranged, the two of us went out, first to dine and then to dance. I knew that my father was not happy, and that he was thinking about having to return home without me. My mood was pensive and I had no appetite to enjoy my meal as I felt guilty about disappointing my father. Oldo was gentle and attentive, witty and passionate all at the same time, and soon his charm and ardour changed my mood and I began to enjoy the evening. The restaurant was elegant, the food and atmosphere delightful, bearing in mind the circumstances of the aftermath of war. Soft music played as the waiters attended the tables and each table had its own telephone. I even had a call from an admirer at another table asking if I would care to dance with him, if it would not offend my companion; Oldo, in fact, was not at all happy about the request! It was all so romantic and exciting, but I naturally declined. Oldo continued to declare his love for me and said he wanted to take care of me for the rest of our lives. I was moved by his words as he spoke of the consuming flames of his love for me. He was caught in a whirlpool of passion, he said, the like of which he had never felt before. I listened to his youthful declarations of love in a trance. Although much younger than he, I felt at that moment older and wiser. In him I saw a reflection of my soul, and within me stirred memories of Alex. I responded with equal passion. Being held in his arms as we tangoed was an intoxicating experience. It was like fusion of two souls. After all the horrors of my childhood, life was suddenly very beautiful. We were together and locked in a moment of enchantment. We spoke of our future, and Oldo proposed to me. When would we marry? In two or three years' time, he said, he should have his doctor's diploma. We could marry then, should I still want him. It was impossible for me not to return his love, he said. I was overwhelmed by his words. Although I did not at that time have marriage in mind, for I was too young, I did not wish to hurt or disappoint him. I was deeply touched and thrilled to have had my first marriage proposal. Oldo looked at me with imploring eyes waiting for an answer. My reply was precipitous: "Oldo, I am Jewish".

I sensed an immediate shock inside him, which he tried to conceal. I felt rather than saw that a shadow had crossed his handsome face. I suddenly felt a chill. I was no longer the love-struck girl of a moment ago. I still must have loved him, but now I observed him somewhat coolly. It must have been the most embarrassing moment of his life.

Oldo was a young progressive democratic Czech patriot. He had every reason to hate his country's former oppressors, and he abhorred Nazism. There was no trace of any anti-semitic feeling in him, yet the very word "Jewish" seemed to have struck a deep-rooted chord in his subconscious. Was it the result of an all-pervasive anti-semitic propaganda which over the years had affected everyone? Or was it merely an uncontrollable manifestation of a centuries-old dormant anti-semitism? I had neither the time nor the desire to analyse his instinctive reaction to the word "Jewish". An invisible gulf seemed to have opened up between us.

Possibly he did not realise the depth of my sensitivity. He kept on telling me how much and how passionately he loved me. I had no doubt that he meant every word of it at that moment. He was trembling for fear of having offended me, and he must surely have sensed something of my awareness, for he became ever more charming and attentive. I pretended not to have noticed his reaction and his desperate efforts to overcome its effects. The temperature had dropped. The mood had changed. A question mark had been placed against our relationship. The feeling of elation was gone. I was no longer the infatuated young girl responding to Oldo's love with abandon. I did not feel hurt, far from it. Rather, I felt proud. I had become proudly conscious that I was Jewish. Oldo had helped me to remember, and to re-establish my identity.

I did all in my power to bring back the mood of only a few moments ago. I did not want Oldo to feel guilty and miserable. I agreed to go on to another night-club with him. He was happy that I had shown no signs of being offended. He wanted to assure me of the strength of his feelings.

"I am ready to be converted to Judaism if you wish, Agnes," he said. But he said it with a smile, almost as a joke.

I made him feel that all was forgiven. In fact, there was nothing to forgive. He had meant no offence, but how could he have known how I felt?

Already I was thinking ahead. When our evening began, I was determined not to return to Budapest with my father. Now, I was thinking the reverse. Oldo would not even suspect. He was happy and gay, scintillating in his conversation. He was excellent company.

It was three o'clock in the morning when he took me back to the Alcron. He told me that he would come to collect me on Monday morning and take me to his parents' villa. I could stay there as long as I wished during my next school year. He even waited in the street until I leaned out of the window of my hotel room and waved him goodnight. I watched as his taxi started and moved off towards the market place. I began humming a tune, perhaps just a little too brightly, to prove to myself that it was all over. If was false gaiety and I knew it. I felt the need to take a hot bath. This done, I went to bed and slept. Deeply and dreamlessly.

In the morning I told my father that I would return to Budapest with him after all. A perfect gentleman, he asked no questions, obviously sensing that something had happened the night before to make me change my mind. He telephoned reception to order my ticket. Whilst we were waiting there was a knock on the door and a beautiful bunch of roses together with a box of chocolates were presented to me. Chocolate was such a luxury in Czechoslovakia at that time, only available on the black market. A card was attached to the flowers, wishing me a day filled with happiness. I looked at the roses and thought of tomorrow. Oldo would call for me at the hotel but I would be far away in Budapest and, I was certain, away from him for evermore. Instead of being heartbroken I wondered a little at my own detachment. Had my former life made me cold and hard? I, who was usually so soft and sentimental, now felt completely unemotional. I felt no regret at the episode of the last few days, on the contrary I was grateful to have experienced something I would not have missed for the world.

For a second time within a year I was heading homewards to Budapest and my mother. As I sat with my father, his body comfortingly warm next to mine, I thought back to the previous journey I had made with him. I had been filled with excitement then, anticipating the meeting with my mother; now I felt a mild detachment due, I am sure, to the events of the night before. I had fallen in love and for a brief, wonderful spell had felt like a fairytale princess. Now it was over and I was leaving my charming prince forever.

I was happy going back to stay with my parents, although I did not feel truly at home in Budapest. I visited friends, went out in the evenings to see the new plays and concerts, and carried on a normal life with my family. Yet I was unsettled. Something was not quite right. There were too many bitter memories here for me, and too many faces from the past reminding me of them. I knew that my parents wanted me to be with them, and I felt that they needed me near. Nevertheless an idea which had been forming in my mind for some time now began to come to the fore more frequently. I wanted to go to Israel. In Israel I could be openly proud of my heritage. I would not have to think about how people were going to react towards me; I would be at one with them. The more I thought about it, the more I knew that this was for me and eventually I voiced my feelings to my parents. At first they were very distressed, and there were many emotional scenes with my mother crying at the thought of losing me again. She had lost her two children and regained one. Now, I wanted to leave. My father appeared to see the logic of my decision and eventually, after much discussion, agreed that it was the right thing for me to do. Meanwhile, I felt that without me my parents might adapt better to post-war Budapest. In time, my father might even regain his old job.

I had heard that passage to Israel could be arranged — albeit illegally — from either Czechoslovakia or Austria. I made a few enquiries and discovered that the only way for me to return to Czechoslovakia was by the border route used by illegal immigrants. I could not ask for legal documents and a passport from the authorities, for it would be obvious to them that I did not intend to return, so I said nothing about my plans to my friends in case word got round. I did not want any of my actions to put my father's job or position in jeopardy, so I told my parents the minimum of details about my plans. I was to "jump the bushes" as it was called, a term used for those leaving as it were, "by the back door". For me, a new life was about to begin. A new horizon beckoned me. What lay ahead was unknown, but what was certain in my own mind was that I wanted my freedom. Whichever path I followed would be of my own choosing, and God would be my guide.

CHAPTER 10

Flight

My second journey to Czechoslovakia was not as simple as the first one. Then I had all the legal documents necessary to allow me to live and study there. Now I was without passport, without a visa and was in fact intent on entering the country illegally. It was to be an eventful journey and not without danger. My "Guide" was a peasant who made his living by smuggling unfortunates across the Hungarian border, showing them the route which would be the least dangerous. I had less to fear than most in this particular circumstance, for as I was a Czech citizen, I felt confident that, should I be captured, the guards would not send me back as I had genuine identification and could provide names and addresses of relatives well-known on that side of the border. Nevertheless I wanted to avoid capture, if only to spare my parents further distress. My father accompanied me to the nearest border town carrying my suitcase and offering last-minute advice. He tried to arrange for the safest possible route, but not having any connections with the smugglers, and working only on recommendation, his choice was nothing more than guesswork. Our farewell was brief. Saddened by the parting my father suddenly looked much older than his years. I embraced him quickly, anxious to be away, and told him that as soon as I reached my destination I would ask my uncle, his brother, to get word to him of my safe arrival.

It was nightfall when I joined my so-called guide, an elderly Hungarian. He was accompanied by a middle-aged couple making their way to Vienna, both very frightened and on the edge of hysteria. So much had happened to me in the past that I no longer had feelings of fear — only of expectancy and urgency. Also, in my youthful ignorance, I failed to appreciate the fact that they possessed no identification papers whatsoever, they were much older than I and were risking much more in their attempt to be re-united with their children in Austria. We exchanged polite greetings and proceeded to listen to the guide's instructions. First we should leave our belongings with him for safe keeping. We would be given them when we reached the other side. Of course I never did regain my suitcase. It was stolen by the guide.

It was cold, dark and windy when we set out. We waited in a muddy ditch near a railway line, hidden by bushes, waiting for our guide to give the word to follow. The sodden earth was like a quagmire, sucking me down into its clammy depths. I took off my shoes to make walking easier. My feet were well used to walking without shoes in extreme conditions. I had stumbled through snow, rain, stones and gravel, starving and weak through sickness and exhaustion, a mere child bewildered and afraid. Now at least, I was healthy and strong, better equipped to face the impending ordeal.

The middle-aged couple were overwrought. She was crying hysterically saying she could not walk quickly enough. Suddenly we heard the barking of dogs and we all stopped still, hardly daring to breathe. Our guide told us to drop down and hide amongst the undergrowth to avoid discovery by what was probably a border patrol. We lay there covered in mud, not daring to move, for what seemed like an eternity. The blood was pounding in my head and my heart was racing as though it would burst.

At last he gave the all-clear and told us that nearby was his friend's cottage where we could clean ourselves and pay for a meal before resuming our journey. The house was on the Czechoslovak border close to a railway station where we would take a train on to another town. We arrived at the cottage and cleaned and tidied ourselves as best we could. I heard the guide talking to his friend telling him to take us at daybreak to the station where he should tell us to crawl under the stationary wagons to avoid being seen, and then to make our way to the main road which was close by. As they were speaking in Czech they assumed that we did not understand their conversation, but I understood every word and did not like the sound of their plan. It was too dangerous. Three people crawling under the wagons would easily be spotted.

As dawn filtered light onto the fields I noticed a narrow river with a bridge in the distance. One side of it was Hungary and on the other side I could see Czechoslovak guards patrolling, and the bright Red, White and Blue colours of the Czechoslovak flag fluttering gently in the early morning breeze. I realised then that we were actually on the border. Probably the guards were so used to seeing this inconspicuous little house that they never thought to search it for escapees. Either that or they had some kind of arrangement and turned a blind eye. I made the decision then to make my own way across the border, and not follow the guide's instructions. Without further thought I ran across the fields to the river, my blistered, swollen feet scarcely seeming to touch the ground. Crossing the river was a bigger problem than I had anticipated. Although quite narrow, parts of it were deep, and my aching legs and feet struggled to keep a hold in the mud and stones of the river bed. It seemed that for every step I took forward I slipped back two. Eventually when I reached the far side and tried to crawl up the bank, my hands and feet just slid back down into the soggy earth. I thought that I would never reach the flat fields as I clawed my way up and out. It was lucky that I had no luggage with me to hamper my progress still further, though had I been carrying anything, I would have surely dumped it. I had learned a long time ago that life was more important than possessions. I eventually managed to haul myself up the bank onto terra firma where I sat a while to regain my breath and to examine my situation. I was covered in mud, my feet were blistered and swollen to double their size, but I was amazed to see that my stockings were still in one piece! No holes and no ladders! Looking around I spotted in the distance a little house and I set out towards it. The further I walked, the further away the house seemed to be. I listened for the sounds of dogs and looked out for guards; always careful, always cautious. Fatigued both mentally and physically, I at last reached the door of the little house. I will always remember the face of the peasant lady who answered my knock. She was a stout woman with a warm beauty about her face, but now she looked worried and somewhat afraid. I spoke to her in Czech and her face relaxed a little. Then I knew that I really was on the Czech side. At first she did not want me to enter her house, but when I explained to her that my uncle lived in the nearby town and that I had enough money to pay her if she could get me to him, she took me inside and gave me food. I cleaned myself and explained more about my uncle, and noticed a sudden change in her attitude. My uncle had a little shop where he sold material and by coincidence she knew him and had often purchased things from him — coupons permitting! She at once bade her husband go fetch my uncle and they returned a short while later in an old car to collect me. The lady was well pleased with the material she received from my uncle in return for the kindness she and her husband had shown me.

I rested and recovered at my uncle's home, and also bought myself a new dress. I asked my uncle to find out what he could for my journey to Israel.

My starting point was to be Bratislava (Presburg). I had attended school there and had seen Germany's ex-Führer at that very place so many years ago. It was from the same school that the Breha, the Zionist Underground, made travel arrangements for stateless refugees wishing to make their way to Israel. When I arrived in Bratislava I looked up a family whom my father had saved from almost certain death during the occupation by furnishing them with false Aryan papers. Their own children were now grown up and married to important government officials, and I could tell that they were not happy to provide shelter for a refugee. My desire to reach Israel by whatever means caused them additional embarrassment. They seemed to forget that they owed their very existence to the unselfish actions of my father, actions which were then also illegal and highly dangerous. Under the circumstances, however, they could not refuse my request to stay with them for a short period, so there I stayed. I gathered together all the news and information I could about the Breha and how they helped stateless Jews reach Israel. Transporting these Jews across Europe was a long, complicated and hazardous operation and the school, now converted into dormitories, had been requisitioned for the use of the would be immigrants. As one group of refugees left another would take its place, so there was a constant flow of human traffic passing through the school "hotel". Life was risky, uncomfortable and difficult for these poor people. Some succeeded in reaching their destinations, others failed. I could not quite understand how it came about, but some of the trains carrying the refugees would proceed with the full knowledge of the Czech government; others less fortunate would be ordered to return to their point of departure taking the hapless human cargoes with them. When I had collected all this information and was sure in my mind of what I had to do, I told the family that I would be leaving their household and travelling on to stay with my uncle. They were relieved to hear of my intended departure, and happy I am sure, when I eventually left.

Meanwhile during my visits to the Breha, I had met a young man whom I shall call J. He was handsome, intelligent and one of the main operators organising the journeys and routes to Israel. He seemed to be someone of importance within the organisation, and I was flattered when he asked me to join his team and help him. As I spoke Czech, Slovak, German and English, my language skills would be of great value, apart from which, he said I was cute, pretty, and just the person he needed! He was not forceful in his approach but spoke with a gentle persuasiveness. I knew little or nothing about the working of the Breha; what I did know was that it was helping Jewish refugees reach a land they could call home, away from the horrors and memories of the lands of their birth. I thought about my own position. I was no longer in danger; I was healthy and able-bodied and I decided that if I could, I would help these people in their quest for peace of mind and security. I told J. that I would join him; whether I would have the courage and stamina needed remained to be seen.

I told the family with whom I had stayed that I was now on my way to see my uncle who was a Rabbi. Instead, I joined J. and started another important chapter in my life. Often during my time working with the Breha, I was to wonder what had happened to the middle aged couple with whom I had started my escape journey. Did they eventually reach Vienna, and were they re-united with their children? I was never to learn the answer.

CHAPTER 11

The Breha

It was obvious from the start that J. was attracted to me. Although he was constantly surrounded by women it seemed to me that he did not socialise very much. He was quite a good-looking young man. Slim build, medium height, with very blond hair. His finely chiselled face was heightened by large blue eyes and something about his appearance reminded me very much of Oldo. He was always very neat, clean and well-dressed, points which always meant a great deal to me. I discovered that he came from Transylvania, on the Hungarian border, and consequently spoke Hungarian but did not understand Czech. Because of the seriousness of his work he afforded little time to girlfriends and formed few close friendships. Many of his contacts were of dubious character, and even the officials he encountered could only be trusted with reservation. He was deeply involved in his work, and had a genuine concern for his fellow Jews and their efforts to reach the new Jewish State. The more I saw of J., the more apparent it became that there was a mutual respect between us. I was extremely flattered to know that he liked and trusted me, and I was pleased to think that I might be able to help him. He and his colleagues did all they could to help the unfortunate refugees who were crammed into the school dormitories. Despite the obvious dangers, each person involved was putting his freedom at risk. After my experience of forced internment, of deprivation of all rights and possessions, my own freedom was very dear to me. I never did understand the politics which deprived a man of his right to live freely. Hitler deprived millions of this basic right, then the British arrived, freed the persecuted wrecks of humanity and released them from a living hell, only to deprive many of those to whom they had given hope, of their right to settle in a new homeland — Palestine. The camps set up on Cyprus were certainly not the concentration camps of Germany; they were nevertheless prisons, from where escape was still impossible. My desire was to help everyone to achieve their goal and reach their destination. I had no political aspirations and wanted no personal gain. Everything I did was solely on humanitarian grounds. Having suffered so much myself as an innocent child, I was determined to do all I could to help others avoid the suffering I had endured.

In Bratislava I met many people, friends and associates of J. who were also giving time and effort to help others less fortunate. I obtained new Czechoslovakian identification papers, and moved and travelled always in the company of J. Because of the kind of work in which we were involved, it would have been dangerous to have a permanent and therefore traceable address, so arrangements were made for us to stay at the biggest hotels in town. The reason for this was simple, albeit devious. A friend would book a room for us in a fictitious name, pay for it and book us out the following day. Another colleague would repeat the process in a different name at the same hotel. In a large hotel where people were coming and going all the time, this was not too difficult an operation. J. would see people in a room, say on the third floor, then by moving to another room the next day, he ensured that he would not be traced should someone start checking up. It was quite an exciting period, and although I never admitted it, there were times when I was truly frightened. I frequently travelled to the border myself to collect people, sometimes alone, sometimes with J. or another colleague, depending on whether the job was to be a big or small operation. We would travel back from the border either by train or bus, sometimes even by taxi, but always in a small number. I never took more than a handful of people at any given time, travelling mostly to villages to meet groups en route to Vienna. Most of the time these manoeuvres went smoothly, but on a couple of occasions I was stopped and questioned. Only my command of both the Czech and Slovak languages saved me.

One occasion which turned out to be quite a frightening experience was when I was travelling to Bratislava with three women passengers. I had hired a taxi with a Czech driver, explaining to him that we were going to the hospital as one of the passengers — my cousin, I said — had appendicitis. The driver was doing his best to get us there quickly urged on, no doubt, by the bottle of vodka which I had proffered. Suddenly, that which I dreaded most happened. We were stopped by the police! In that dreadful moment before they approached the taxi, I thought that my heart would surely burst. Gathering together all the feminine charm I could muster, I smiled sweetly at the officer and jokingly mentioned that I had a bottle of vodka with me, primarily for medicinal purposes as my cousin was in pain and on the way to hospital. However, as it was such a cold day, if he should care for a quick nip to warm himself, then I would gladly spare him that much before we hurried away. Returning my smile, he declined my offer, said a few words in Czech and wished me luck with my patient in the back of the taxi. As we drew away, we breathed a sigh of relief and after the ordeal we had just been through decided that WE needed the nip of vodka! As I passed it to my passengers, I realised that although they had probably been very anxious as to what might happen, they had most probably remained calm during the ordeal because all they had seen were smiling faces. Not understanding Czech, they had been unaware of the nature of the conversation, and as everything looked so relaxed and friendly, they had remained calm.

On returning from each mission J. would be there anxiously waiting for me. It was obvious that his anxiety was for more than just the success of the mission. He was becoming more and more attached to me as time went by and I could see that he really did care for me. Apart from the clandestine operations which he organised, the only other responsibility J. had was me. I was so involved with helping J. I forgot to write to my uncle, the Rabbi, to let him know that my arrival would be delayed. I had failed to communicate with either him or my parents for some time, although the one family member I had managed to speak to was another uncle whom I saw quite regularly when I visited the border on my illegal trips. I had asked him to tell my parents that my trip to Israel was being delayed for a while as I had met a young man whom I would introduce to them later. I described J. as best I could, explaining that he was presentable, a few years older than I and that he was a good friend and companion. I said nothing about his work, only that I was safe and secure in his company. Whether or not the correct information was conveyed to my parents I shall never know. Whatever messages he did pass on left my parents in a state of uncertainty about my well-being. My Rabbi uncle, also worried, took it into his head to seek me out and to find out for himself just what was happening to me. This was no easy task, for as I have explained we were careful to leave no traceable address. However, perhaps because of his influence as a Rabbi, he did manager to gather information about me, and the knowledge that I was living in a hotel with some young man pleased him not at all! He was not to know that our relationship was purely platonic — if only because I wanted it that way — and he was not unnaturally worried. I was totally aware, of course, that J. was in love with me, but as yet, I did not return his feelings. Because of the mutal trust and respect which we shared, and also perhaps because he was careful not to rush me, J. was always a gentleman towards me and treated me honourably. I think he knew that should my feelings for him change and become deeper, then when I was ready, I would let him know. It was a situation which many, certainly my uncle, would not have comprehended. All that mattered to me though was that I was happy and that my own conscience was clear.

Arriving one day at the hotel reception area, I glanced around looking at the day's visitors and to my horror recognised my uncle. Although my uncle had not seen me in years the shock reaction on my face told him that he had found his niece. There he was, all clean and dignified, his dark beard combed and shiny, waiting for me to arrive. I could not believe my eyes. J. saw the shock register on my face and immediately thought that I had seen some sign of danger. I realised that a meeting there and then could very well prove dangerous for J. and our organisation, so I quickly explained who the imposing looking Rabbi was. J. agreed that the hotel was no place for a meeting, and suggested that we go to an office in the school dormitory to have a proper discussion. Once there I received a severe rebuke from my uncle. Although quite fair minded, he refused to be liberal about my sharing a room in a hotel with a man who was not my husband! However worthy our work in the Breha, he still found our relationship totally unacceptable — and said so. He calmed down when we told him that all was not as he had assumed, but he insisted that I return with him and stay at his home until I decided what I was going to do. If J. should wish to see me he could visit me at any time, but should we wish to travel to Israel together he would only allow it if we were married! So to avoid making more problems for either J. or myself I agreed to return with him to Brno.

Brno was a pleasant little town which I grew to like very much. I also liked the idea of once again being part of a family, and my aunt and uncle were extremely kind to me and made me most welcome. I realised that I had missed the warmth and unity of family life, and that I needed very much to be a part of it. For so long I had been surrounded by strangers and short-term acquaintances. Now I began to appreciate again the meaning of the word "family". My new home was very comfortable and I settled in quickly and happily. My uncle had also suffered in one of the concentration camps — Auschwitz. One day his group leader had told my uncle that there was another member of the working party for which he was responsible who came from the same town in Czechoslovakia. When he could manage to slip away from work, my uncle sought out this man and started to ask him questions. The staggering truth was revealed some minutes later when the two men realised that they were brothers! Their physical condition was so appalling, so emaciated, that they were totally beyond recognition!

My stay in Brno was a happy one. I contacted my other uncle who lived near the border, told him that I was safe and well, and asked him to convey the news to my anxious parents. The next problem was my wardrobe. My aunt was a smart well-dressed woman and I was clothes conscious, so she took me to the best "haute couture" dressmaker in town. I remember years later wearing those dresses I had made — they were of such good cut and quality. Living with my aunt and uncle was a totally different experience for me. Very different from the life I had been leading with J. Being religious they did not socialise very much or entertain.

My uncle wanted to know what my intentions were towards J. and what plans I had for the future. I was confused. I was not really sure that I was doing the right thing, but I eventually consented to marriage with J.

I decided to make the most of my stay and to enjoy myself as best I could. I was in no danger, and was no longer living in a state of tension and anxiety. Here I could relax for a while and lead a normal life as a young healthy woman should. I went shopping with my aunt, made a few new friends and had the occasional telephone call from J., keeping me up-to-date on what was happening in the Breha. J. was delighted at the proposed marriage and was planning to visit me shortly. I lived day to day, making tentative plans for the future wondering if I had made the right decision about J. Deep in my heart I knew that for me this would be a marriage of convenience. My family would not allow me to travel to Israel with J. unless we were married. J. understood my feelings and although he was obviously pleased with the idea of marriage, he did promise that should I wish it, we would have the marriage annulled in Israel. I still had doubts in my mind, but at the time it seemed the only thing to do. J. planned to wind up his work and affairs as quickly as possible, then we could be married and go to Israel to start a new life. J. visited me on several occasions, each time fortunately without mishap. He was confident in his manner, posing convincingly as a Slovak, and encountered no problems crossing the border. I felt sure that were he to meet with trouble or have the misfortune to be questioned, his many friends and contacts would have rallied round to save him from imprisonment. Maybe I was just being optimistic, but happily my optimism was never put to the test.

Originally our wedding was planned for the Spring but as the situation for J. became more and more dangerous, we advanced the date. Later, we went by train to the Viennese border hoping to make the first step of our journey to Israel, but we were turned back. Fortunately some of the officials knew J., and instead of arresting us merely advised us to return home. There were many difficulties in those days for stateless refugees, and trains were often turned back from Bratislava and instructed to return to their point of departure. It was distressing, to say the least, for those who had made the journey, hoping to start a new life and leave behind all the past tragedies and heartaches. Most of the people had little money and no jobs to return to. Even so, with the odds stacked against them, they tried again and again to cross the border, and eventually some did achieve their new life in Israel. As always, when people meet a crisis, some are able to draw on an inner strength.

Because of his contacts and connections my other uncle who lived on the border was able to obtain a pass for me and my new husband to visit my parents, this time quite legally. My mother and father were also given a pass, which meant we could meet openly, and I could introduce them to J. By a strange quirk of fate the bridge where we met was none other than the one which, some time earlier, I had used as an escape route across the border! We were escorted by a Czech guard across the bridge and there, separated by a long pole barrier, I made the introductions. I was very happy to see my parents again, and they in turn were happy to know that I was safe and well. They had asked permission to give me a gift and they handed me an envelope containing some money. They appeared to be quite satisfied with J. and happy that we were going to Israel as man and wife. I still had doubts about the arrangement not the least concerning J's ability to settle down to a normal life after the tension and excitement of his former work. The prospect of family life, however, appealed greatly to J. although apart from a brother and sister-in-law in Romania, he had no other family. We said our goodbyes and parted somewhat sadly, promising to let my parents know when we arrived in Israel. I wondered how long it would be before we would see each other again.

After the failure of our first attempt to cross the border to Vienna, J. decided we needed a vacation so we went to the elegant ski resort of Poprad. It was a popular place and very beautiful. Some of the scenery was quite breathtaking. Apart from the many visitors who came to sample the ski slopes, it was also a place where people suffering from tuberculosis came to convalesce, and there were several sanatoria in the area. Although a complete novice at skiing, I enjoyed myself immensely. Despite the cold and the snow, the blazing sun gave me a healthy tan, and we would sit in the pretty little chalets chatting with people we had met, drinking mulled wine and admiring the splendid scenery. Although I was happy there I was by no means entirely relaxed. After living in a state of constant suspense and anxiety, due to the possibility of arrest, I was still unable to feel completely at ease. The police still used to drop in unexpectedly at the hotels and ask for identification, and although these occasions passed without problem, I was always ill-at-ease and nervous. This aside, I was thrilled to have my first holiday in years.

One day J. wanted me to go for a walk with him to the woods. I was not very enthusiastic, as walking was not one of my favourite pastimes, but to please him I consented to go. J. was very artistic and able to use his hands well. As we were walking, he cut down a slim bough of tree and with his pocket-knife started to whittle and carve. Over the next few weeks, whenever he had an odd few minutes, he would whittle away, carefully, painstakingly forming the wood into a beautifully fashioned walking stick. Every inch had some pattern carved into it and he told me that he had carved it just for me, and that much of himself had gone into its making. His eyes were shining when he presented it to me, and I knew that it meant much to him. Even so, I was unable to show him the appreciation which it merited. I was later to regret not having received it with greater enthusiasm. I kept the stick for many years, but somewhere, somehow, it was lost.

Sometime during our holiday word came to J. that our papers were ready and that at the end of our three weeks holiday we should make our way to Bratislava from where we would travel by train to Vienna. We both began to feel excited about the forthcoming journey, and with mounting anticipation we said goodbye to the friends we had made. We set off for Bratislava, and there met friends of J's who wished us a safe journey. This time it seemed that luck was with us, and we were not turned back. We arrived at the beautiful city of Vienna without encountering any problems. I felt that I had seen Czechoslovakia for the last time.

CHAPTER 12

In Transit

When at last we arrived in Vienna, I relaxed. Now I felt safe and no longer afraid. J. had friends there who received us with warmth and courtesy. For the first time in years I felt free. Freedom seems so much more precious when one has been denied it, and I savoured my freedom with great zest. We were taken to a camp set aside for Jewish refugees wishing to make their way to Israel. It was a sort of "half-way house" providing accommodation and food before the final journey. J. and I were given 'better-than-average' quarters within the prefab-type buildings which were sparse but clean and comfortable. We were given a small amount of pocket money, and I decided that I would like to see the sights. My previous visits to Vienna had been fleeting; now I wanted to see at my leisure the beauty of this ancient city. I wanted to walk through the old streets with our new friends, stop at the friendly bierkellars and coffee houses and enjoy my liberty in normal, happy surroundings. But all too soon my expectations were dashed. Because accommodation in the camp was limited, and the stream of new arrivals endless, we realised that we would have to move on as quickly as possible to make way for the next batch of refugees. So my hopes of some leisurely sightseeing were squashed although I did manage a couple of short shopping expeditions. Vienna like the rest of Europe was suffering the after-effects of war, and the shops only had a limited selection of goods to offer the would-be purchaser. In spite of — or perhaps because of — the harsh memories of the war, people went about their business and leisure with a freshness and vigour so different from the depressing uncertainty of recent times, almost as though they were determined to be happy, taking what pleasure there was to be had, and enjoying every moment to the full. J's friends were very kind to us but nevertheless they wanted us to be on our way. Arrangements were made for us to travel by bus to Salzburg, and my uneasiness and anxiety were fuelled yet again by the news that there could still be danger ahead. To reach the American sector we would first have to cross the Russian zone. Everyone was briefed on how to behave, and those people like myself who spoke Slav languages were particularly warned about remaining silent. Our "guide" would do the talking as and when necessary, for we were to be classed as "sightseeing tourists". I suddenly felt as though my world was about to fall apart. I thought that I had earned my freedom, yet there were still hurdles to overcome before freedom would really be mine. The stress and strain of all that had gone before seemed suddenly to catch up and overwhelm me and I felt that I could take no more. In this state of extreme nervous tension I broke down and cried. All the hurt and humiliation, the pain and suffering poured out through my tears. When would it all end? What had I done in my young life that I had to atone in this way? My strength seemed to drain away and a feeling of desolation enveloped me. J. was very kind and understanding and his friends full of sympathy and comfort. It was rare, they said, for anything serious to go wrong or for anyone to be turned back. Just a little more patience, just a few more precautions, then we would truly be free. So, once again I rode the path to freedom. We sat for what seemed like hours on the bus, each with his own private thoughts and hopes. My heart was pounding with fear as I clutched the packed lunch bag given us for the journey. J. did his best to calm me, talking softly and gently about our plans for the future.

When we stopped suddenly and I read the notice "YOU ARE NOW ENTERING THE RUSSIAN SECTOR", I thought that I would faint. There was a stillness on the bus as we waited. It was as though everyone had stopped breathing simultaneously, waiting for some judge to pass sentence. Two Russians dressed in civilian clothing entered the bus. One went over to the driver, the other made his way around the seats of the bus, stopping at each passenger and looking closely into his or her face. As the Russian approached me, I looked directly into his blue eyes, noting his typical Slav features. He smiled a sweet, gentle smile, reminding me of the inviting smiles I had seen on the faces of SS guards before they inflicted some horrendous torture on their terrified victims. Then I remembered. These men were our liberators not our captors. They had freed us from the Germans, they were not like them. I had to stop thinking of the past and judging everyone by German SS standards. Suddenly my confidence returned. As he looked at me, still smiling, I smiled back. He moved on, said a few brief words to the driver, then with his colleague stepped off the bus and was gone. It was over. I breathed again and sank back into my seat, weak from tension. We had made it! Someone called out that we were still in the Russian sector but that soon we would reach the American zone. By the time we arrived I was feeling decidedly ill. The tension and fear had played havoc with my nerves and I felt about as strong as a newborn kitten. As the American control let us through a cheer passed everyone's lips and as if by magic bottles of vodka, wine and other spirits appeared, and we drank, old and young, clinking the bottles to celebrate our success. The bus echoed with the sounds of joyful singing voices mingled with tears of relief and happiness. Songs were sung in Polish, Russian and Czech as each nationality celebrated its freedom. Then as the ultimate salute began, and everyone stood to sing the Israeli National Anthem, a reaction set in and I began to cry. The blood was pounding in my head, the singing seemed to get louder, then distant, and I almost lost consciousness. I was aware of J. holding my hand and his anxious voice soothing me, telling me it was over. I looked around and saw everyone embracing; then I took a deep breath. The air of freedom.

The splendour of Salzburg never failed to enchant me, and our arrival in that beautiful town filled me with excitement and wonder. To me it seemed like a fairytale setting etched in gossamer and lace. The houses, the castles, the lakes and mountains all had a beauty of their own, an indescribable aura I have yet to see repeated. Salzburg was special. It was beautiful, it was enchanting, and it was the gate to freedom.

Once again we were taken to a camp where we were received by one of J's best friends. We were afforded an extra room in the barracks, and our first meal was followed by a warm friendly reception. J's friend welcomed me with true affection; knowing that I now belonged to his friend. I left them talking and making plans as I settled down in my bed mentally and emotionally exhausted. Before I went to sleep, I let my thoughts linger awhile. I did not have to worry about tomorrow — that would be a fresh start, a new day. From now on I could live like a normal, human being, not having to look over my shoulder all the time. I could learn to enjoy life and people. Every moment would be mine to do with whatever I wanted, whenever I wanted.

I awoke the next morning with a great sense of contentment. Relaxed, I pondered over all I had gone through, and the events which had led up to our arrival in Salzburg. Now, at long last, I was to start the new life I had for so long dreamed about. I had already started planning my future. How I would dress and wear my hair; the places which I would visit, even the kinds of food I would eat. At breakfast J. said we would go into town and he would buy me some new clothes. Then we could do some sightseeing and visit whatever places that I pleased.

At first, I enjoyed Salzburg, visiting the town with J. and his friends. They warned us of the impending difficulties and setbacks we might encounter in Israel, but their words did not dampen my enthusiasm. After the hardships I had endured so far, whatever crisis might occur could be no worse than those which I had survived. Typhoid, bullets, disease and starvation had been unable to claim my body and soul. Now nothing would stop me from reaching my destination. I feared nothing and no-one, and I had in my possession the two essential factors to carry me through: my health and my freedom.

I began to notice a gradual change in J. I had wondered before how he would adapt and adjust to our new way of life, no longer having the excitement and the danger of his previous commitments. Now that he had me as a dependant and a responsibility, and life followed a more "normal" pattern, a change of attitude became apparent. At first I rebelled and feelings ran high. Then I kept my opinions to myself, determined not to allow the situation to make me unhappy. The atmosphere between us became more strained, and I felt that J. was no longer the close friend and companion of yesterday. Our relationship continued on a slightly less even keel.

In Salzburg there was a lovely coffee-house which we used to visit and sometimes J. or his friends would treat me to the delicious cakes that were sold there. After one visit, we were standing outside looking through the window display for some purchase I wanted to make when we were suddenly rounded up by the police on one of their "black market" raids. Apparently there were a lot of "black market" dealings in the area being carried out by various refugees and we were unfortunate enough to be caught up in this latest round-up. The effect on me was traumatic. Again the police, again the questions, and again the searching. We were totally innocent, yet we were being examined and searched like criminals. I started to cry. "I thought I was a free person," I sobbed. "Why am I being searched?" Both the policemen and policewomen were sympathetic towards me, and when they turned out my handbag and saw the collection of rubbish it held, they realised that I was innocent. What they had not seen was the handkerchief bundle which I had removed! Inside that, wrapped in a paper serviette was the money which my father had given me on the bridge in front of the border guards in Czechoslovakia. Had they found it and questioned me there was no way that I could have proved that it was a wedding present. Even J. did not know about it. That little bundle of money was my independence, my lifeline. If I ever again reached the point of starvation, that money would help me to buy bread. The memories of total deprivation were very vivid and I had a deep-rooted need to keep something in reserve for times of adversity. We were released with an apology but told that these sudden raids were necessary and would continue to be carried out. The incident unnerved and unsettled me and afterwards I no longer felt at ease to enjoy the beauty of Salzburg. J. tried to reassure me, but the damage was done. All I wanted now was to leave and reach Israel as quickly as possible. There, I knew my relatives would welcome me, I would not be alone, and I would have no need to look over my shoulder every time I walked down a street.

Then came the day of our final journey to Israel. We were taken by bus to the harbour where we boarded a boat which would take us to Haifa. Excitement surged through my body at the thought of what lay ahead. For the first time in weeks, I began to feel uninhibited relief. Although material possessions had never meant a great deal to me, I began to take great delight in the most childish of trinkets; anything bright and colourful pleased me. I sensed that J. was not altogether pleased by my sudden effervescence and that he was jealous of my child-like innocence, resenting his own inability to share in my exuberance and delight. I gained pleasure from such simple things, having been deprived for so long from the joys of life. I felt nothing but jubilation for the future. To me it was going to be an adventure. I was on the brink of something wonderful and I was determined not to let his attitude spoil my happiness.

Ahead was a new life in a new country. Israel was waiting for me — and I was on my way!

CHAPTER 13

Freedom

The journey to Israel was quite comfortable and pleasant, and the food — when I was well enough to eat it — adequate and nourishing. Unfortunately I was seasick more than once and on these occasions I stayed in my cabin just sleeping and resting. For the remainder of the time a happy atmosphere prevailed amongst the passengers with the crew and captain joining in the dancing and singing. Every nationality seemed to be assembled on that boat, all closely bound in a common unity. There was a feeling of togetherness, freedom and lighthearted camaraderie. It was as though our shackles had been unlocked, and now life and limb were free. I very much enjoyed those few carefree days when everyone was looking forward to the same horizon.

As we neared the shores of Israel, a feeling of mounting excitement pervaded the boat. Everyone was scanning the water for the first glimpse of the land which would give us back the right to live as human beings. So much hope and faith were directed towards that little piece of God's earth. Earth which for centuries had been fought over and wept over, and which had soaked up so much of the blood of suffering and torment. And then suddenly — there it was. The most beautiful, welcoming sight in the world. The port of Haifa. To me in these first few wonderful moments it looked like a glamorous French resort, Cannes or Monte Carlo. I was amazed at how modern it appeared. As the boat steered towards the dock side, I took mental photographs of the panorama before me, pictures which, even now, I can recall as vividly as though it were yesterday. Outlined against the clear blue skies I could see the slopes of

Mount Carmel and the golden dome of a building I learned later was set within the beautiful Persian Gardens. It was a scene of peace and tranquility and I experienced a profound feeling of awe. Looking around me I saw my fellow passengers embracing each other in joy and happiness, with tears of heartfelt emotion pouring down their faces.

J. took hold of my hand, and as I looked up at him I saw tears in his eyes too. I wondered why. Was he afraid of the future and his responsibilities, or were the tears for the memories of the past? Whatever the reason, he was deeply touched by his own thoughts of the moment. As for myself, I was too happy to shed tears. I gazed bright-eyed at the blue sea, the clear skies and the slopes of Mount Carmel, lush and green in the sunlight. I was bewitched, engulfed in an aura of happiness, and a joy I shall remember to the end of my days.

The decision to come to Israel had not been a simple one as it involved a further separation from my beloved parents. I had taken a big step in order to start a new life for myself. Now at last I was here. "Next year in Jerusalem" is the prayer of every Jew, and circumstances of horror made this prayer into a reality. Here the "yellow star" was a symbol of hope and freedom, and here every Jew could walk with his head held high. As I looked at J. and the shining faces before me emotion welled up inside me. Each and every one of us knew what Hell was; we had all lived through it. But we had survived. Here was our salvation, here was our freedom, and here at last was our Promised Land.

EPILOGUE 1982

More than thirty years after the manuscript for the book was completed the following event happened.

While travelling through Scandinavia on holiday with my eldest son, we were told that instead of stopping overnight in Hamburg on the return journey, the coach would stay one night in Hanover. HANOVER! The place where I had lived after the Liberation in the care of Major Chutter! Memories flooded my mind, and I began to cough nervously. Would I have the courage to visit number 40 Bardowiker Street? By the time we reached the hotel at seven that evening I had decided to revisit my old dwelling place. My son was against my going, fearing that the painful memories would upset me, but I had made up my mind. A lady teacher from Kidderminster, on our tour group, insisted on accompanying me, so after a quick supper we stepped out into the rain and hailed a taxi. I asked the driver if he knew where the street was, and after consulting his map he told me it was the other side of the city, and that the fare would be expensive. I told him I was here only for one night and briefly explained the reason for my visiting the place. To my surprise and consternation tears welled up in his eyes, he was visibly overcome with emotion, and he immediately stopped the fare meter! Full of heartfelt regrets and apologies he said he would drive me anywhere I wanted, free of charge, and that he was at my disposal! The next few minutes were quite hair-raising as he drove zigzag through the rain blinded by his own tears! My companion even offered to drive the taxi, so afraid were we of crashing! However, the driver regained his composure and began to ask question after question. He had never seen or spoken to any child who had been in a concentration camp. What was it like?

Was it really as bad as the books and pictures showed? Why did the inmates respond so readily to every order, however degrading? I explained that the image of the Jews standing when told to stand, jumping when told to jump, being still when told to be still, was true. We acted like robots because to do otherwise could mean flogging or death. A twitching finger or the blinking of an eye was enough to enrage a Nazi officer, and give him (or her) the excuse to give vent to sadistic impulses. When someone has a gun pointing at you, you do not ask questions — you obey.

For two hours he drove us around the old city showing us everything and plying me with questions. He was a good-looking man of 40 and I drew from him a genuine feeling of dismay and revulsion at what his fellow countrymen had done. Their guilt lay heavily on his shoulders. For my part I had previously categorised all Germans into a "uniform type" conforming to the ideas of my youth. This man changed my feelings that evening.

We drove past the Town Hall where Major Chutter had had his offices, but numbers 40-42-44 Bardowiker Strasse were no longer there! I had intended knocking on the door of number 40 and explaining who I was and the reason for my intrusion, but now this was impossible I had to admit to feeling a sense of relief. Our driver used his car radio to call his office to ask if anyone knew what had happened to the villas. Yes, they knew. The three had been acquired after the Liberation by the allies as homes for the young refugees, the owners having been paid compensation for giving up their homes. Later they were sold, and the land acquired for another purpose. Now, in place of the three villas stood a hotel! My visit over, the driver invited us to his home, but as my companion and I were anxious to return to our respective sons, we declined his offer.

Back at the hotel I reflected on the incongruity of the past few hours. I, the one who had suffered and was battling with painful memories, had been comforting the taxi driver through HIS tears and anguish! My inner strength had enabled me to give strength and comfort to another.

APPENDIX

The Liberation of Belsen

ACKNOWLEDGMENT

The very helpful assistance given by the Ministry of Defence in permitting extracts to be made from the booklet "The Story of Belsen" published in 1945 by 113 L.A.A. Regiment R.A. (DLT) T.A. (100 A.A. Brigade) is gratefully acknowledged.

THE TRUCE

On 12 April 1945 following the break-through of Second Army after the Rhine crossing the German Military Commander at BERGEN-BELSEN (Chief of Staff 1 Para Army) approached 8 Corps with a view to negotiating a truce and avoiding a battle in the area of Belsen Concentration Camp.

In occupation of the area were 800 Wehrmacht, 1,500 Hungarians with their wives and families, and certain SS Prison Guards. In the Concentration Camp were known to be 45-55,000 internees of whom a very large number were reported to be suffering from Typhus, Typhoid, Tuberculosis and Gastro-Enteritis. The electricity and water supply had failed: there was no bread and very little food.

THE TASK

About 50% of the inmates were in need of immediate hospital treatment. All of them had been without food for 7 days, and prior to that living on the normal concentration camp semi-starvation scale of diet.

There were about 10,000 typhus-infected bodies, mostly naked and many in an advanced stage of decomposition, lying around the camp, both inside and outside the huts, which required immediate burial; and the daily death rate was 4,500.

The living conditions were appalling — people were sleeping 3 in a bed, mainly treble-bunk beds, and huts which would normally accommodate 60 were housing 600. There were no sanitary arrangements, and both inside and outside the huts was an almost continuous carpet of dead bodies, human excreta, rags, and filth.

There were some 50,000 persons to supply and feed, but the cooking facilities were totally inadequate. There were 5 cookhouses of varying size equipped with a number of large boilers, and the only containers available to distribute the food were a few large dustbins. A large proportion of the occupants were bed-ridden, and many were incapable even of feeding themselves.

BELSEN' PURPOSE

Belsen was a Krankenlager or "Sick Camp". It was not in any sense a hospital camp nor do prisoners seem to have been intended to recover. In the other Concentration Camps it was openly stated by their Commandants that anyone who went to Belsen would not come back; among their inmates a transport to Belsen was regarded as the last journey. Although the Camp had been established before the War, no witnesses have been found who have been there longer than 8/9 months and the majority have only been in the Camp for 3/4 months. There was no gas chamber as at the even more infamous camp at Aushwitz, where according to numerous testimonies hundreds of thousands were done to death by this means. Starvation, disease, and physical degradation were the lethal weapons employed at Belsen. It would appear that the purpose of Concentration Camps was to eliminate whole sections of the population. Two limiting factors deterred the Germans from doing this immediately on arrival of the prisoners. First, they wished to benefit by having in their power hostages for the good conduct of those left behind. Second, immediate destruction would have stimulated much greater resistance. It is quite clear that what took place in all the Concentration Camps was not intended to be mere incarceration, but was destruction either immediate or delayed.